Images Of Silver

Left:

Afternoon – Upper Mataura. A deliberately under exposed shot transforms an afternoon scene into an evening one.

Images Of Silver

A Guide To Back Country Fishing

The Ultimate Trout Fishing Experience

Les Hill & Graeme Marshall

The Halcyon Press

Published by
The Halcyon Press.
A division of
Halcyon Publishing Ltd.
C.P.O. Box 360, Auckland, New Zealand.

Printed through
Colorcraft Ltd,
Hong Kong

Typeset by
Typeset Graphics

ISBN 0-908685-24-6

Copyright © Les Hill & Graeme Marshall
First Published in hardcover 1993
This limpcover edition first published 1998
Reprinted 2004
All Rights Reserved

All the photographs were taken by Les Hill. All the text was written by Graeme Marshall apart from the chapter on still waters and the introduction.

No part of this publication may be reproduced, stored in a retrieval system or transmitted in any form or by any means, electronic, mechanical, photocopy, recording, or otherwise without written permission of the publisher.

Contents

ACKNOWLEDGEMENTS		6
INTRODUCTION		7
CHAPTER ONE	The Back Country Experience	9
CHAPTER TWO	Angling Through The Seasons	19
CHAPTER THREE	Stalking: The Back Country Method	37
CHAPTER FOUR	Back Country Fishing Technique	55
CHAPTER FIVE	Fishing Still Waters	80
CHAPTER SIX	Conservation and Preservation	101
BIBLIOGRAPHY		120

Acknowledgements

This book has been some time in the making. I applaud Graham Gurr, our ever-faithful publisher, for his confidence in us. Once again I salute my co-author, Les Hill. Unless one has fished with him it is impossible to describe his generosity, unflagging good humour and sheer love of his sport. These photographs are the result of years of constant striving. For him second best is not sufficient. My family must receive mention again, if only for accepting my periods of non-communication and solitary confinement without demur.

Graeme Marshall

When taking the photos for this book I required the assistance of many anglers. I am most grateful for the tolerance of the following people who endured the lens of my camera continually pointing their way – or who stood or cast in an appropriate place (while there were fish waiting elsewhere) so that a particular scene or mood could be captured.

Sincere thanks to: Ho Hill, Tim Varley, Len Cook, Jack Taylor, Graeme Marshall, Terry Marshall, Alan Pannett, Jill Dyer, Philip Sanford, John McDowell, Frank Sullivan, Norman Moody, Eden Shields, Tony Allen, Chappie Chapman, Brian Smith, Doug Ives, Rex Devine, Mike Howell, Lou Franklin and Grant Winter.

Les Hill

Introduction

'Images of Silver' creates in my mind pictures of clarity, vividness and sparkle; pictures of luxuriance, vitality and purity; things to be desired, treasured, valued to the utmost.

In angling terms it portrays crystal-clear waters, deep green pools and sparkling ripples with margins of flourishing forests or grasslands, crimson-flanked rainbows and fat, speckled browns; places where the only sounds are the dawn chorus, the rustle of a breeze in the trees or insects voicing their presence in the heat of the day. The angling too has shimmering qualities – thrashing fish, dripping lines, smiling faces and the honesty of solitude. They still exist, those sparkling places.

In this book we have tried to show the qualities of the back country we enjoy. In the first part, the rivers themselves are, to the discerning, vastly varied. Snow-fed streams glisten opalescent while rainfed neighbours emit emeralds and greens of infinite subtleness and depth. Some mountain streams tumble, seemingly endlessly over huge boulder beds while others meander through primeval forests over beds of mud and silt. Towering mountains, snow-topped and awesome look down on some, while others lie open, tussock-lined, to prevailing wind and squall. All lie awaiting discovery.

The fishing exudes vitality and effervescence with finesse and delicacy too – all of which we have tried to capture. Awaiting an angler can be endless hours of excitement – of sneaking through bush, crawling along grassy banks or peering over rock bluffs, of a return to camp in the dark through just looking round one bend too many, of fish with proportions one need lie less about and whose fight ensures they get away.

In the back country anglers are at their best as people. The greyness, through pressure of everyday life and work is gone. The silver and freshness of anticipation prevails.

In portraying these qualities we hope that our readers see them too – see them as they exist today but more importantly envisage their fragility. These places of silver sadly are sought not only by those who seek pleasure alone wishing to take nothing else (not even the fish) but by others after more tangible gains. They are sought by those who wish to lower the forests, leaving lands of brown and rivers the same, those who wish to build dams of grey or waste paddocks of mud and yellow, those who dispose wastes of red and orange – all to extract the greenness of the dollar.

    The golden days of New Zealand angling have passed. Some silver still exists. We see it as worthy of preservation for New Zealanders now and in the future. We hope you see it that way too.   LES HILL

CHAPTER ONE

The Back Country Experience

In his book *Trout and Salmon of the World*, Silvio Calabi describes New Zealand trout fishing thus: 'The finest brown trout fishery on earth, in terms of a high-quality angling experience that often yields a beautifully marked 5 or 6 pound (or 8 or 10 pound) fish each day, is probably New Zealand's.'

In this book we record, in words and pictures, something of the lesser-known parts of that fishery – the remote regions of the South Island. It is certain that the book will heighten interest in back country fishing. Above all though it is our hope that it will bring a message of conservation so that New Zealanders and visitors alike will work together to preserve as well as enjoy.

To many American anglers, back country is synonymous with high country. Most of the more remote streams in the western United States are indeed located at high altitudes in the arid areas of Colorado, Montana or Wyoming, for example. Many visiting anglers, therefore, are surprised to discover that many of our prime back country rivers are less than 100 metres above sea level. For us, back country means a degree of remoteness rather than height above sea level, and remoteness is something the South Island of New Zealand still offers in abundance.

Streams and rivers, with populations of wild self-sustaining brown and rainbow trout, flow from the hills and mountains virtually down the whole length of the island but there is no doubt that the best fishing is found away from the land clearing efforts of man. While the rivers on the plains frequently run dirty for many days after heavy rain, the mountain headwaters remain relatively clear during heavy floods and drop with a rapidity that never ceases to amaze.

A typical trout stream on the western side of the great alpine chain will have its origins in rock and tussock high above the tree line. Some water may be held in alpine tarns before spilling over into the lush rainforest below. Initially the myriad of tiny rivulets rush and tumble through the forest, often dropping hundreds of metres in a series of waterfalls and rapids. The streams soon meet others, frequently rushing through narrow gorges before suddenly spilling out onto quite extensive alluvial flats. There may be some fishable water here but the back country angler is more likely to be found among the pools further back in the hills.

Eastward flowing rivers often have similar origins but the forest (mainly beech) is

Right:

For the fit only, in the heart of Fiordland. Geologically young country with rivers tumbling through monstrous boulders, precipitous gorges and dense virgin forest.

Left:

Crossing the lower Eglinton. The lower Eglinton can be negotiated at low flow – JUST!

Below:

A John Morton mayfly. John Morton is a well known Christchurch angler and fly tier. Each of John's flies is a work of art.

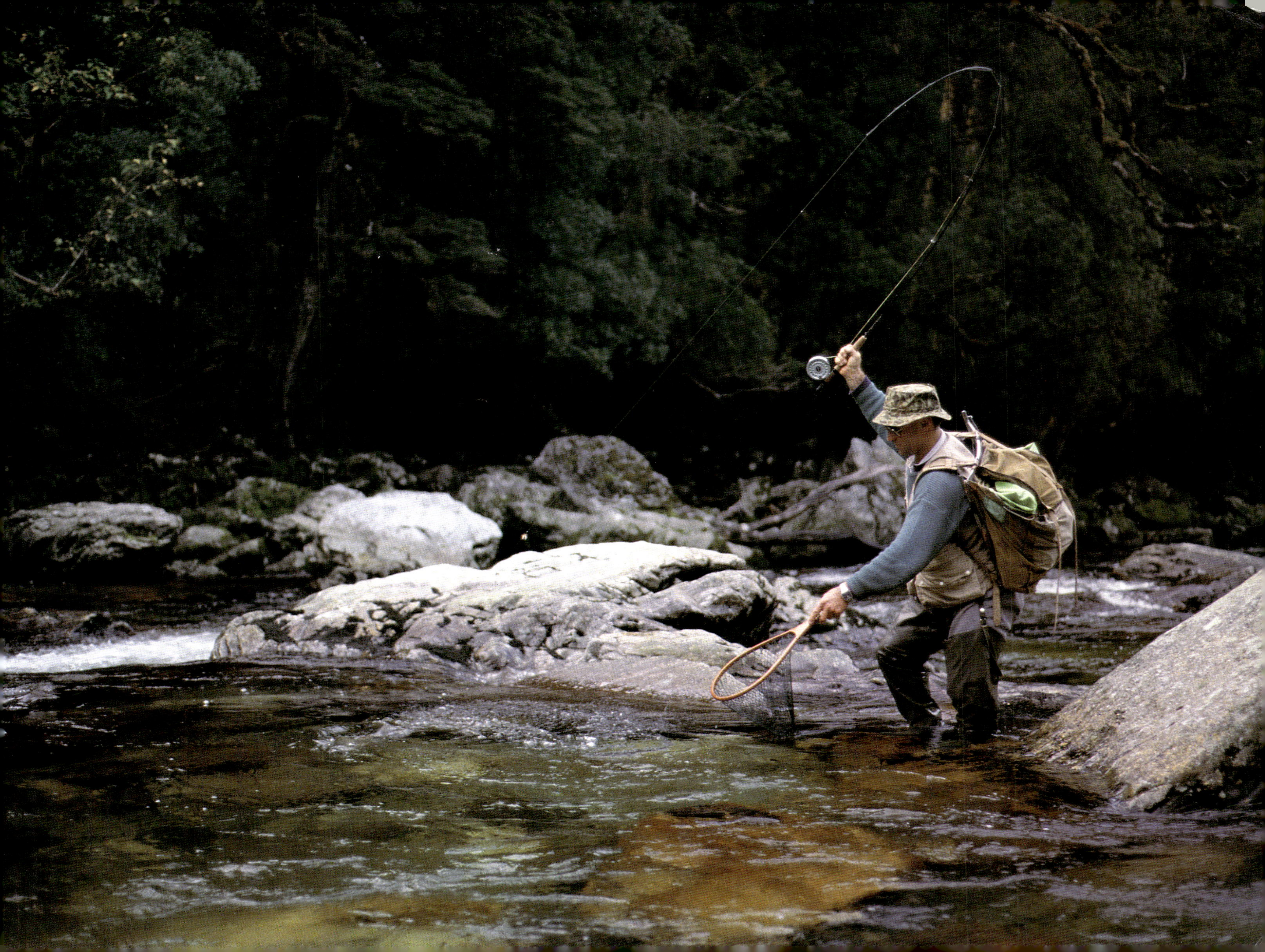

noticeably more open and drier. All too quickly these rivers spill out onto a wide, braided flood-plain, although in Otago and Southland there are some real gems which flow unfettered for many kilometres in largely one channel. Fiordland rivers often descend in a series of steps and, although the valley sides are neck-wrenchingly steep, the valley floors are relatively gentle, especially as they approach the sea.

Lakes, ranging in size from perhaps a hectare or two to vast inland waterways abound from north to south on both sides of the great divide. While the rivers have deservedly received more attention, perceptive anglers do not overlook the still waters. In the west, you will find lakes set amidst lush, almost tropical looking forest whereas on the drier eastern slopes there may not be a tree for many kilometres, but, don't be fooled – the streams flowing through those barren, often windswept areas may contain fish of astounding size and quality.

The weather plays an important part in all this. Strong westerly winds regularly fling their loads of rain and snow at the western slopes of the alpine chain. So the river flows are maintained and the high country lakes in the east, on which we depend for much of our hydro-electric generation, are fed. Over 7000mm of annual rainfall is quite common in Fiordland and South Westland, while, on the eastern side of the divide, only a few kilometres distant as the crow flies, less than 400 mm a year is sometimes recorded. So diversity is the hallmark of back country trout habitats - diversity of terrain, vegetation, rainfall and temperature.

Although liberations of ova and fry have been carried out throughout the country over many decades many of the more remote streams have been stocked by entirely natural means; the trout having strayed into river systems during excursions along the coast. It is now considered likely that most brown trout in some river systems spend at least part of their lives at sea. While some may not venture far from the stream of their birth, others are thought to travel quite long distances. While browns frequently run to sea there is little evidence to indicate that rainbows are so inclined.

There was a time when the South Island's rivers and lakes were the preserve of a small number of local anglers. Today it is a different story. The superb back country opportunities have been discovered by overseas anglers. Quick to capitalise on this burgeoning interest have been entrepreneurial lodge owners, travel agents and guides. While even as recently as 1980 only a very few guides operated on more than a casual part-time basis; now scores are making guiding their main source of income. Some have formed their own organisation - the New Zealand Professional Fishing Guides Association - a body determined to maintain the highest possible standards as befit the quality of the resource. Few areas of the country with good trout streams are without at least one member of the association, and others who choose not to become members.

As Silvio Calabi points out, to fish in New Zealand, and particularly in the back country streams accessible only by helicopter, 'requires deep pockets'. Quite so. The sums expended on accommodation, helicopter and guide fees on the top of the cost of getting here and internal transfers, are astronomical in the eyes of the average Kiwi wage or salary earner. That the anglers continue to come - from the U.S., Japan, Britain and a range of European countries - is testament to the quality of the experience.

Calabi, in commenting on why so many travel so far at such great expense, says, 'It is still marvellous by most standards and the setting is unsurpassed anywhere on earth. I believe New Zealand is the only place on earth that I have never heard a single complaint about from a travelling fisherman.'

While there may be an element of exaggeration in that last statement for many trips are thwarted to at least some degree by the unpredictable weather and the sheer contrariness of the trout, he is probably not too far short of the mark.

If one questions visiting American anglers closely after they have fished for big back country browns and rainbows their comments usually run something like this;

The scenery/river was just gorgeous.
The water is so clear.
We just don't see big trout out in the open feeding in bright sunlight. Don't the fish have any predators apart from man?

Right:
First light on Lake Manapouri. Manapouri lies nestled among high glacial mountains. When the sun first peeps over the tops a moody morning light is produced.

Bush country magic. A beautiful, jade green, West Otago stream yields a fine trout.

Above:
The Quarry. A magnificent, well-conditioned Otago brown just netted.

14 Images of Silver

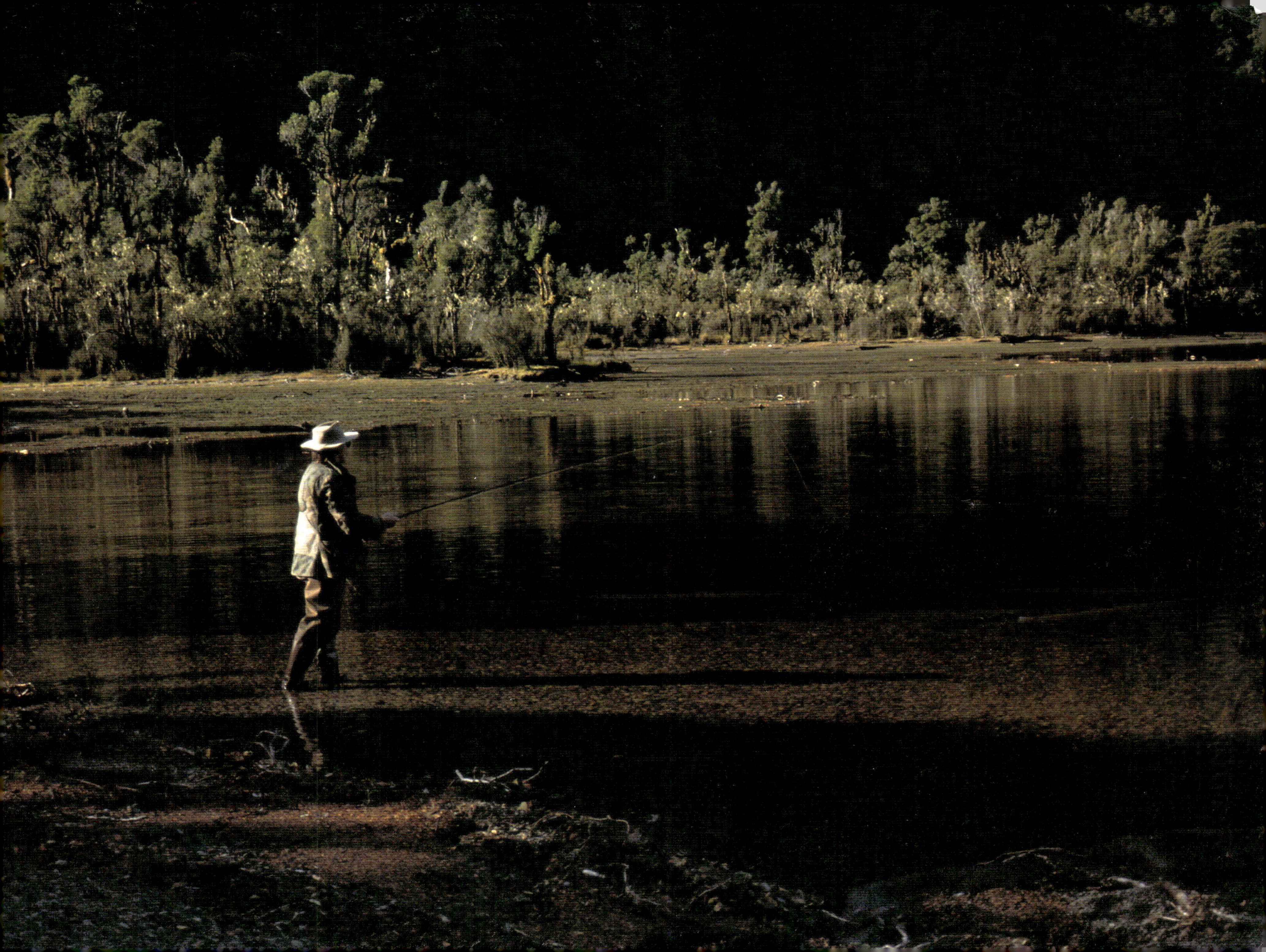

I never believed that I would see a 3 kg trout take a dry fly in sunny, clear conditions.

Our browns are sedentary and nocturnal by nature. You very rarely see them out in the middle of the day. The only way you'll get them is by throwing a fly right under the bank or log where they are hiding.

These fish are such great fighters. Our browns are often long and thin and don't put up much of a scrap.

Your fish can be so spooky. I could have caught up to 30 or 40 small rainbows up to 40 cm on my favourite stream at home but I love the challenge of stalking and spotting fish before casting to them, even if I only landed two all day.

It's the 'stalking' that fascinates many of them. The technique, which is second nature to most New Zealanders, is a source of much intrigue for the majority of visitors, and seems to have captured their imagination to an astonishing degree.

The sheer size and quality of trout available in the South Island back country obviously has tremendous appeal. Few reasonably competent anglers, especially with the help of an eagle-eyed guide, will fail to land at least a few trout in the 2-3 kg category, and even an occasional fish over 4 kg. For many any brown trout over 50 cm long would represent the trophy of a lifetime; yet these are relatively abundant.

It is plain that quality rather than quantity is the keynote. True, on an exceptional day 15 or even 20 fish over 2 kg, especially where rainbows predominate, is possible, but in the main, even the most experienced of Kiwi anglers would be content with perhaps 4 or 5 fish landed in an 8- or 10- hour fishing day. Part of the reason for this lies in the fact that some streams hold very low numbers of large and exceedingly wary fish. The nature of the terrain, especially on the rougher West Coast rivers, militates against even the keenest and most physically fit of anglers. Frequent river crossings, rough travel over huge boulders, and inevitable detours into the near impenetrable forest limit fishing opportunities. Some streams may hold only a few catchable fish per kilometre, so it is little wonder that even helicopter-borne anglers may have the opportunity to fish to fewer than 10 trout in the course of a full day's fishing.

Late Autumn sun on Te Anau. In the cool of May, first sun on chilly waters often produces a surface mist – a photographer's delight.

Indeed, some, who equate angling success with numbers of fish in the net are a mite disappointed, but in the main these are people better suited to the volume fisheries of Alaska or Chile where sometimes it is possible to hook huge rainbows with virtually every cast. South Island back country fishing is rarely easy, often frustrating in the extreme and beset by the limitations of an imposing physical environment. Yet, once you are 'bitten by the bug', the challenges become almost addictive as you seek to explore exciting new waters. It is this element of mystery which drives the back country angler on and on in anticipation of encounters with fish of mythical proportions.

Fishing the back country is also a levelling experience, for even the finest of anglers experience the occasional 'blank' day, most frequently at times of very high or very low water flows, or as a result of excessive fishing pressure. Few fish can be as sensitive to the presence of man as the brown trout. Many anglers would scoff at the suggestion that some browns will become almost uncatchable if fished to often enough.

We can attest to the truth of this bold statement. The browns of the heavily fished Mataura or Motueka are so accustomed to disturbance from anglers, swimmers, rafters, kayakers and jet boaters that in order to survive they must resume feeding quickly after being alarmed, albeit a little more warily, and probably in a less accessible part of the river.

In the main this maxim does not apply in most back country waters. With increasing pressure browns in particular may not be available to the stalking angler for some days, or at least feed in a state of considerable agitation, remaining on station in feeding mode for the briefest of periods, and constantly alert to a heavy footfall, clumsy movement, rod flash or just the tiniest splash of a weighted nymph contacting the surface of the water. If one thing is for certain, it is that the challenges are not going to diminish unless the trout become more accepting of the invasion of their territory, and of being caught and released on numerous occasions.

For those prepared to accept the challenge of difficult terrain, inclement weather and perhaps the spookiest trout on the planet, the rewards are there, as even the most cursory of inspections of these photographs will confirm.

CHAPTER TWO

Angling Through The Seasons

With the exception of a relatively small number of streams and rivers flowing into lakes (rainbow fisheries in the main) there is a closed season on the middle and upper reaches of most South Island rivers from 1 May until 30 September each year. While some would argue that closed seasons are unnecessary, fishing opportunities being limited by climate and the uncooperative nature of the fish, there is little doubt that the almost total absence of disturbance by man makes for some fine fishing in the early part of each new season. Those who regularly fish in back country areas contemplate each opening day with a degree of anticipation common to sportsmen, worldwide, whether they be anglers, duck hunters or the pursuers of some form of big game. While an 'opening day' is fraught with difficulties in the form of overcrowding, and sometimes boorish behaviour by those who do not understand the meaning of the term 'ethics', it is eagerly awaited, nonetheless.

In this writer's experience the opening day of the trout season only rarely lives up to perceived expectations in terms of fish landed. It is enjoyed and savoured all the same, signalling the beginning of another seven months of fishing opportunities, some in familiar haunts, and many in pastures new. Like the duck hunter barely able to sleep in the nights leading up to the glorious first Saturday in May, any angler fortunate enough to be close to a trout stream on the night of 30 September is barely able to contain his or her impatience.

When I lived in the headwaters of the Motueka River, and was forced to work if the first day of October fell on a week day, I sometimes drove to a favourite stretch late the previous night. After a fitful and restless slumber in the car I would be on the river at first light, determined to be the first through the run. The students in my classes probably suffered somewhat as a result of my weariness, but at least I had the satisfaction of knowing for certain that I had fished virgin water.

Nowadays many anglers seek such water, and it is usually possible to find it, even yet, with planning and forethought. But, even so, early October is often not the most productive of times, especially in the higher and colder areas. Hard frosts still whiten valley floors and in recent seasons the headwaters of mountain streams have been locked in deep snow drifts. Consequently many rivers run low, clear and cold. The trout, responding to the stimuli of

Action on the Wilkin River. Being glacial-fed the Wilkin possesses a characteristically blue hue – slightly milky, cold.

Below:

Just after rain in Fiordland. Following rain as mist still rolls along mountain faces the changing light unfolds an unusual atmosphere.

Lake Heron in winter. When snow and ice clothe our fisheries water temperatures drop to a level required for trout to breed. Such scenes are spectacular yet also essential for trout survival.

Left:
A damp West Coast day – Ahaura River. Despite passing showers and a slightly swollen river trout can still be caught.

Images of Silver 21

longer days and warmer temperatures, are often active for relatively brief periods in the middle of the day until the warm, moisture-laden north-westerlies induce a thaw and fill the waterways with cold, grey torrents of flood water.

The spring floods are a blessing in disguise. Often destructive to the streams and to the farms lower down, they provide the necessary stimulus to encourage the fish to make up for lost time as they strive to regain the condition lost through the rigours of spawning and the lost urge to feed during the short, icy winter days. So the brief clearances which occur during the spring thaw often provide some of the most productive angling of the entire season.

In one river of our acquaintance the best dry fly fishing of the year occurs during October and November as the river is dropping from a major fresh. With the mid-stream current too violent and turbulent for comfort, the fish, browns all, may be encountered literally with backs out of the water amongst stream-side foliage and in the pockets amongst the jumble of lichen-encrusted boulders. As long as it is possible to see into the water it is possible to stalk and fish to individual fish.

One of the wonders of most back country streams is that they rarely remain discoloured for more than a day or two once the heaviest rain has ceased. The trick, of course, is to be in the right place at the right time. Too many early season expeditions have been wiped out by incessant rain, with one front following hard on the heels of another. Such a scenario is common in the spring, especially in western and southern regions. Even if the rain is not falling in the east the rivers will remain unfishable there too because of the rain and the snow melt in the headwaters. Frustrating indeed.

Those opening months – October for predominantly brown trout rivers and November for rainbow fisheries – are a time of considerable movement of fish. Resident spawning fish may have established their territory already but fish which spawned lower down the main stem of the river, or fresh run fish from the sea are likely to be nosing their way up into a pool or run capable of providing the necessary combination of a regular food source and suitable protection from floods and predators.

Early one October I observed many large brown trout feeding actively in the shallow tails of pools and in the very skimpiest of side riffles in one back country river. It was clear that these fish were not likely to stay permanently in such vulnerable situations, and subsequent visits confirmed this. It would seem logical to conclude then that the fish were moving in search of more comfortable living quarters. It is likely that the movement is both upstream and down. The headwaters of the smaller tributaries do not hold enough comfortable niches to support large numbers of big fish, and so it is that many must move on. This would explain the often aggressive behaviour of large, male fish at this time, and it is interesting to note, from detailed catch records, that large males greatly outnumber females in most headwater fisheries, sometimes by as much as ten to one. So it is likely that females are much more migratory by nature, in back country streams at least.

It is generally assumed that early season fish are somewhat out of condition. Not necessarily so. In fact we have found that many fish in some headwater fisheries are in better condition just at the end of the winter than they are in the autumn. Obviously some feeding occurs year round despite cold water temperatures. Perhaps the extra effort and the calories expended during the summer months can in fact result in a net loss of condition if a particular fish is stressed by competition for food, and possibly by being put off feeding for quite lengthy periods due to angling pressure. It would be interesting to see some research data on that theory.

Mind you, early season fish do vary in condition. It is at this time when the rigours of spawning and a succession of floods would seem to take their toll – obviously Nature's way of culling old and less useful fish. Occasionally one encounters a very dark fish lying almost motionless on the edge of the stream. Totally disinterested in food dropped literally on its nose, such a fish, if caught often appears to be in decline. In severe cases it is probably kindest to kill it. Dark, lacking lustre, thin and with an outsized head its days are numbered. In many South Island streams it is likely that such fish will be predated upon by shags or eels.

By contrast some early season specimens are in their prime. Hungry and aggressive, these fish are most often found in the optimum feeding zones in the eye of pools, in front of obstructions and in pockets fed by a significant flow of food-bearing water. Often tossing aside

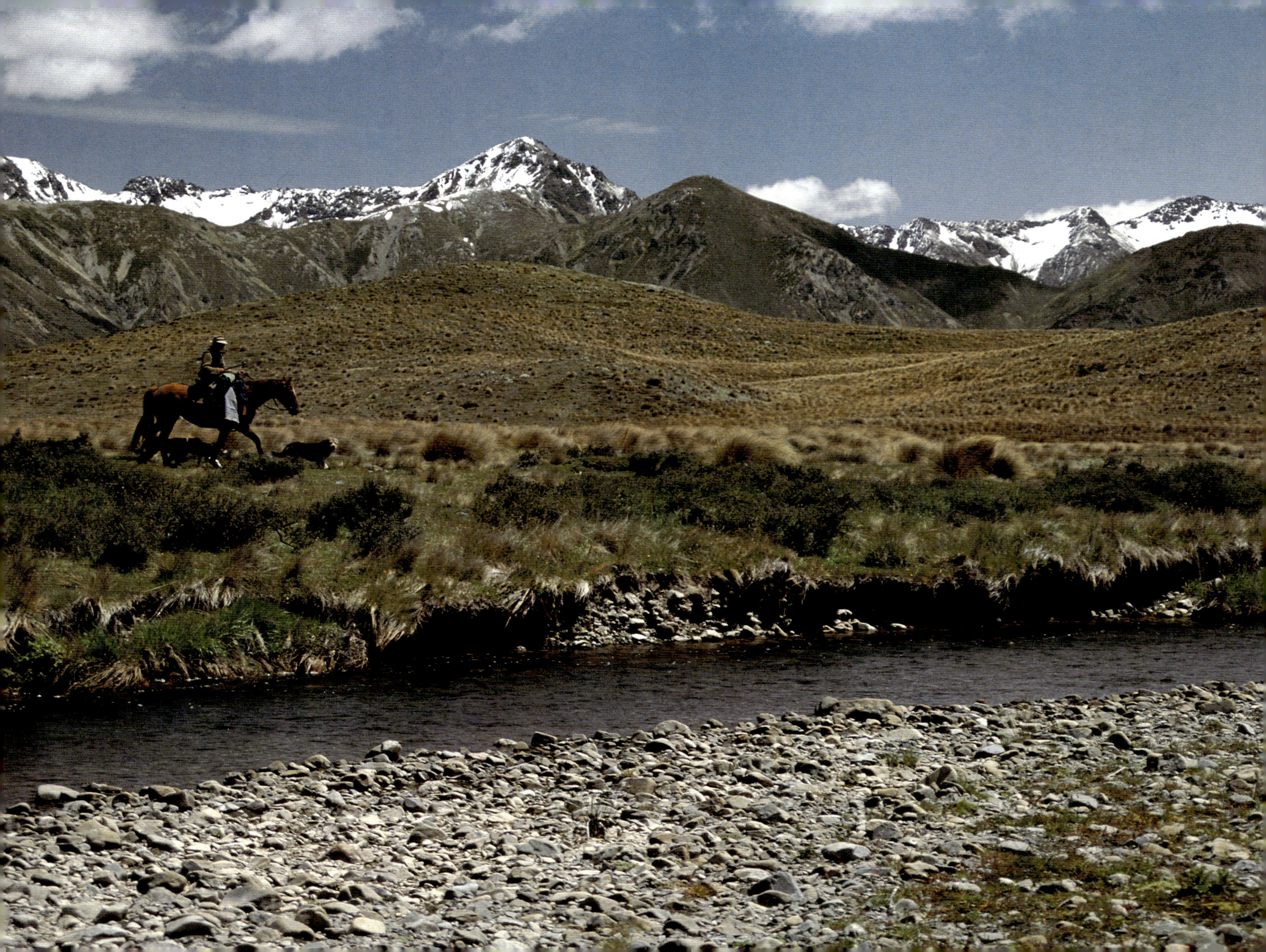

A high country musterer. Fishermen should always respect the property they cross. Permission should always be sought when going onto private land. Horseback guardians are often encountered like this one on the southern boundary of the Molesworth station.

Eglinton lupins. A floral backdrop adding colour to both river bank and water.

Left:
A Marlborough backwater. Fishing backwaters with their deep, clear, still waters requires utmost patience and stealth. However, beneath floating foliage and bankside vegetation some fine trout lurk.

Images of Silver 25

their natural caution, these fish are the epitome of back country trout, the dream-makers with catholic tastes and forgiving of minor errors in casting technique or careless approach. These specimens are to be savoured as their relative vulnerability is likely to be short-lived once the initial feeding lust is satiated.

While the northern hemisphere has experienced unseasonably mild winters and hot, dry summers in the early 1990s New Zealand has suffered from the combined effects of the El Nino effect, a complex mix of unusual ocean currents and wind patterns, and an atmosphere clearly affected by volcanic dust emanating from Mt Pinatubo in the Philippines many thousands of kilometres to the north. Carried by strong jet stream winds in the upper atmosphere the dust was clearly visible, especially at dawn and dusk during 1992.

Farmers in the east of the South Island bore the brunt of one of the most vicious winters in living memory in 1992. A number of snowstorms of considerable duration and blizzard intensity created havoc in the back country. Scores of thousands of sheep, deer and cattle perished despite the efforts of the army and civilian volunteers. For two years in a row Central Otago was gripped in a freeze of almost unprecedented proportions.

Summer, when it arrived was a great disappointment. With temperatures much lower than the norm, cool, cloudy days often accompanied by strong winds, have been the order of the day for a number of summers in the 1990s.

The pattern of front following on front has persisted into the summer of 1992/93. Great temperature fluctuations, and lots of rain have kept river levels high in the main. December is normally beetle and mayfly month on many back country streams and lakes but in many areas cool nights and days seemed to inhibit even the prolific brown and green terrestrial beetles which form a large part of the diet of both browns and rainbows at this time. And the mayflies? Hatches have been conspicuous by their absence on both upland and low country streams of late, or at least so brief and unpredictable that the fish ignore floating duns and concentrate entirely on emerging nymphs.

But what of a normal summer in the back country? El Nino is dying, so we are told, and the Philippine volcanos may settle down for a few more decades. It is easy to find scapegoats for less than perfect fishing. Spells of bad weather have always been a feature of summer in the mountain regions of this country. Snow on the hills at Christmas, unseasonal frosts in February; it is not difficult to cast a thought or two well back beyond the 1990s to prove that inclemency is the norm. While the meteorologists and records insist that the current aberrant weather and temperature patterns are not just a figment of the imagination it must be accepted that anything is possible on a long narrow island sitting square in the path of the 'roaring forties'.

The greatest volume of rain recorded in a 24-hour period at Milford Sound deep in Fiordland was in the month of January. Summer certainly, but recognised as frequently the wettest month of the year.

Browns in particular are wonderfully adaptable to the frequent, high intensity floods which sweep through their homes with little warning. I used to worry excessively about the effect on trout stocks of these dramatic events but now lose little sleep over it. A typical flood was one experienced in February 1992 in the Karamea River, north-west Nelson. The rain, threatening for most of the afternoon, began to fall right on dark; just a few large, sporadic plops at first, but soon beating a steady tattoo on the iron roof of the six-bunk hut. The rain must have had a soothing effect because I slept soundly until around 6a.m. when a cursory glance through the grimy window pane confirmed that little fishing would be done that day. The main river was already big and boisterous, stained a light brown and carrying considerable quantities of debris in the form of branches and even whole trees. Mist hung low, shrouding the dark-hued beech forest and obliterating the mountains completely. A few hours more rest seemed the order of the day.

When I checked again some hours later the level had risen alarmingly and the noise of the river had increased in volume. A closer inspection in an attempt to source the now deep rumbling sound resulted in the realisation that virtually the entire river bed was on the move, the large, round granite boulders rolling destructively downstream. As the day progressed the rain continued to beat down. Our small party took a walk both upstream and down on the track, only to find ourselves blocked by great, gushing torrents of water flowing in normally dry depressions. We retired to the hut and read and chatted for the rest of the day.

The Hurunui yields. The Hurunui is one of Canterbury's best stocked rivers. A playground for anglers, canoeists and rafters alike.

Below:

Hollyford Tributary. The Hollyford River which follows the Milford/Te Anau road in its upper reaches must rate as one of the most spectacular and beautiful in New Zealand.

28 **Images of Silver**

La Fontaine Stream. Probably the West Coast's most celebrated stream. Spring-fed, stable and very beautiful it yields some fine brown trout.

In the late afternoon there was a slight easing of the rain and a glance at the sky revealed swiftly moving clouds rather than the totally motionless grey monotone of earlier in the day. In an hour or so the rain had stopped and almost immediately the water level, which we estimated had risen around four metres in the previous 20 hours, began to recede. By dark the level had dropped by half a metre. Dawn revealed a grey, misty morning but with a hint of blue not far beyond the mist. The Karamea was still in flood, but, amazingly, the level had dropped by at least two metres and a glance at the edge water indicated that rocks could be seen on the bottom 30 centimetres down. To cut a long story short, by 10 a.m. we were spotting fish hard against the bank, sometimes right amongst a tangle of coprosma shrubs, and provided we were able to spot them before they 'saw' us we were able to take them on large dry flies.

Later the effects of the flood became fully apparent. One side stream had been literally blown apart by what appeared to be the sudden breaching of a dam of debris. A small clearing, fully 2,000 square metres in area alongside had disappeared. Everywhere freshly deposited driftwood was to be found tangled in trees and scrub at impossibly high levels, and all this in less than 24 hours.

And what of the trout? In the days that followed we caught fish in abundance. While some showed evidence of scars from some passing rock or branch most appeared totally unscathed. If some fish had been destroyed by the flood I saw no evidence of it. While there was some evidence of congregation in large, deep pools, it was not long before they were nosing back into the shallow pocket water again. This is a 100 per cent brown trout fishery, remember. While rainbows may not have fared so well without the sanctuary of a lake to retreat to there is little evidence to support the contention that even very significant flood events will harm a fishery for long.

Exceptions to this rule occur when a very large slip deposits quantities of fine, insect-destroying silt or sand over the free-stone boulder bed of a river. That happens in Fiordland from time to time and may result in a very poor fishery for some years, or at least until the fine material is cleared away. In the main, though, such events are of relatively short duration.

December is officially the start of summer in New Zealand, and while it may be reluctant to show itself in some years, long, balmy days and a twilight which never seems to wane, especially in the deep south, eventually signal its presence. By then most territorial battles have ceased, and the fish have found their niches, from which many will not stray until the urge to breed overcomes the need for food and security.

Even a week or so with little significant rain will bring about a rapid drop in river levels, especially in the latter part of January and into February. For the stalking fly angler, prepared to hunt for individual fish and try for them with light lines, long leaders and small flies, this is the optimum time. The fish, so easily fooled in the high water of spring are now choosy. Less likely to take an over-large pattern or one which is not reasonably suggestive of a natural, the brown especially becomes wary to a degree which is almost incomprehensible at times.

Even the shadow of a 5X tippet, the tiniest plop of a #16 weighted nymph or the flash of a rod tip during false casting may result in a fish which dashes rapidly to a secure bolt hole, or at the very least ceases feeding and takes on a rigid tenseness as it attempts to ascertain what is wrong.

To the thinking, skilful angler the results will come. The careful cast of an appropriate fly may end with the hooking and landing of a trout of size, grace and beauty. Summer is a time of surprises, of fish to be found in heavy, white water and tempted up by an inviting looking dry; of others found literally at one's feet grubbing around for caddis pupa in water barely deep enough to float them; of encountering perhaps 30 fish in one run porpoising, splashing and leaping clear of the water as they gorge on emerging caddis; of some which suddenly switch from mayfly nymphs to wolf down a huge cicada as it flutters helplessly down a fast run. This and more is the essence of summer fishing in the back country, just as much as it is giving up as a Canterbury 'nor-wester rises in intensity yet a few more notches or watching the Fiordland rain descend in a solid, vertical sheet.

As summer progresses a frontal system to drop some rain and 'freshen up' the streams is often much to be desired. Too much of a good thing soon results in lethargic, 'spooky' fish. The most difficult angling conditions of all frequently occur at the end of a long, hot, cloudless

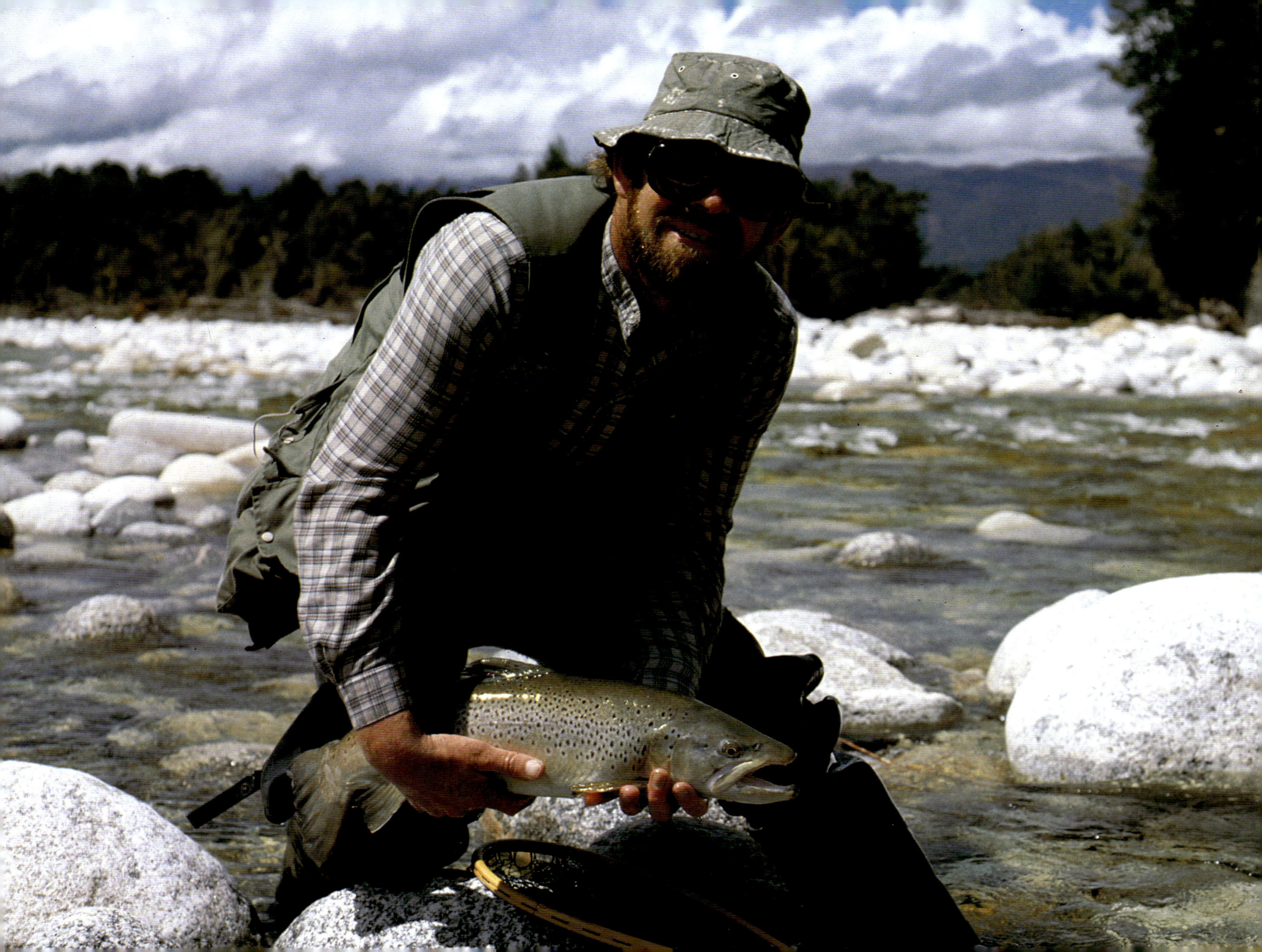

On a rugged West Coast stream. Christchurch fishing tackle manufacturer and fishing guide, Tony Allen, returning a good brown to its rightful place. The immediate background shows a demanding and often floodswept river bed.

summer. Fish retire to the deep, cool pools or are concealed under seemingly impossible rapids. At this time a fresh is most welcome, especially if it raises the river level somewhat, and shakes the fish from their lethargy by providing food in the form of dislodged nymphs and drowned terrestrials. The rise in river level often heralds a welcome hatch of mayflies, inducing a brief but welcome flurry of surface feeding activity.

Perhaps the most difficult angling season in the back country, but sometimes as productive as any, albeit with activity confined to the middle and end of the day, is autumn. Whole stretches of river may appear bereft of fish, while others, which held but a small, stable population earlier, become crowded. Fish are often to be found chasing one another around or massing up in large pods. Shoals of small fish may suddenly appear, patrolling restlessly, moving as one, relying on the security afforded by numbers. Sometimes fish of very large proportions appear in a run which they have not frequented all season, often at the confluence of a tributary stream.

As autumn proceeds feeding becomes more and more tied into water temperature, and this coincides with the afternoons in the main, though a warm rain may result in action much earlier in the day. Typically, late afternoon while there is still sun on the water is an ideal time for a mayfly hatch. A burst of activity for as little as 30 minutes may produce the best fishing of the day, a time to be savoured like a fine wine. Even as late as mid May, rainbows, later spawners than browns, frequently indulge in a feeding binge as intense as any at any stage of the season. This is a time to target the big lake residents which steal up out the vast still waters to satisfy the spawning urge in the side streams of the lake-feeding rivers.

Nature is not foolish enough to allow all spawning to be concentrated in one short time span. Both browns and rainbows spread their breeding over a number of months, typically May to July for browns and July to September for rainbows, though some spawning is quite common outside these months. It is at this time that the future generations are at most risk. A very wet winter may result in constant disturbance of the redds and consequent low survival rate. For that reason alone it is perhaps fortuitous that the cooler years of the 1990s have involved fewer winter floods than normal. From our observations over many river systems the

Right: Lake Heron in summer. Another shot of Lake Heron showing another mood – different yet equally attractive.

A lively Waiau brown. Despite having only a fraction of its former flow the Waiau River still has some interesting semi-wilderness fishing. Beware the recently carved, steep mudstone banks – they're as slippery as ice.

Below:
Californian poppy – common on Canterbury river beds in November.

34 Images of Silver

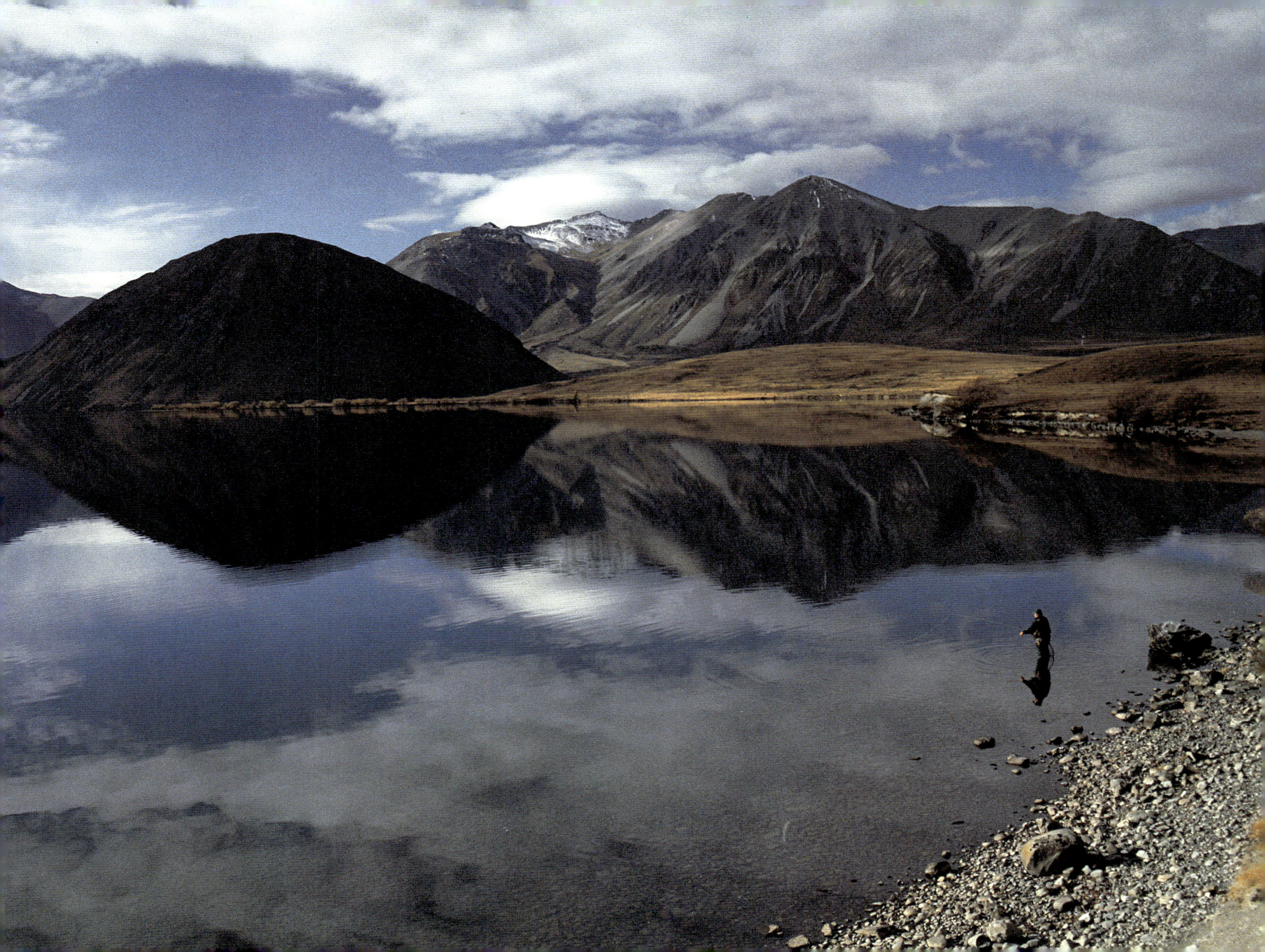

early 1990's have produced some exceptional spawning seasons, certainly a good omen for the years to come.

CHAPTER THREE **_Stalking: The Back Country Method_**

Morning on a river in north Westland. Steep, densely packed slopes clothed in a sombre olive green livery of beech, interspersed with taller, elegant, lighter-hued rimus, still prevent the summer sun from giving light and life to the river chuckling amongst the large, smooth granite boulders. Glimpses of blue through ethereal wisps of mist clinging tenaciously to the foliage give promise of a glorious day after the rain of the night.

We are only days away from Christmas but the air has a decided nip to it, not surprising as a dusting of snow to well below the treeline tells of the intensity of the frontal system which passed rapidly through in the preceding twelve hours.

Little damage has been done to the river though. Although it is slightly discoloured and a few centimetres higher than usual, visibility is still excellent. Every multi-hued pebble can be seen in the deceptively deep water. Wooed by the crisp, clean air and the resonant lilt of bellbirds emanating from the sun-touched higher slopes, the anglers pause a little to drink in the scene, savouring the solitude and harmony of the place. Hearts beat a little faster in anticipation of the action to follow. Donning polaroid glasses and pulling their wide-brimmed hats down firmly, the anglers slip into hunting mode.

In our book _Stalking Trout_ we likened fishing for trout to hunting game animals. We are convinced that this is the correct approach to the problems posed by wild brown and rainbow trout in the South Island back country. Those unused to the technique frequently find a world of angling opportunities opening up especially in streams which hold very low numbers of fish per kilometre. Whilst some U.S. rivers may hold literally thousands of trout per kilometre, for reasons mentioned earlier, most New Zealand rivers hold at best a few hundred and in some cases, particularly in headwater fisheries, less than the number of fingers on two hands per kilometre. It is obvious then that in the main, blind fishing techniques will produce few fish and much frustration. It is encumbent upon the angler to become skilled at reading likely fish holding water and to isolate the most likely lies. With all the will at our command, and no matter how experienced or skilled at the art we may become, some fish will be spooked during the course of virtually every fishing day on a back country river, even though the weather and river conditions may optimise spotting opportunities. The natural protective colouring of a

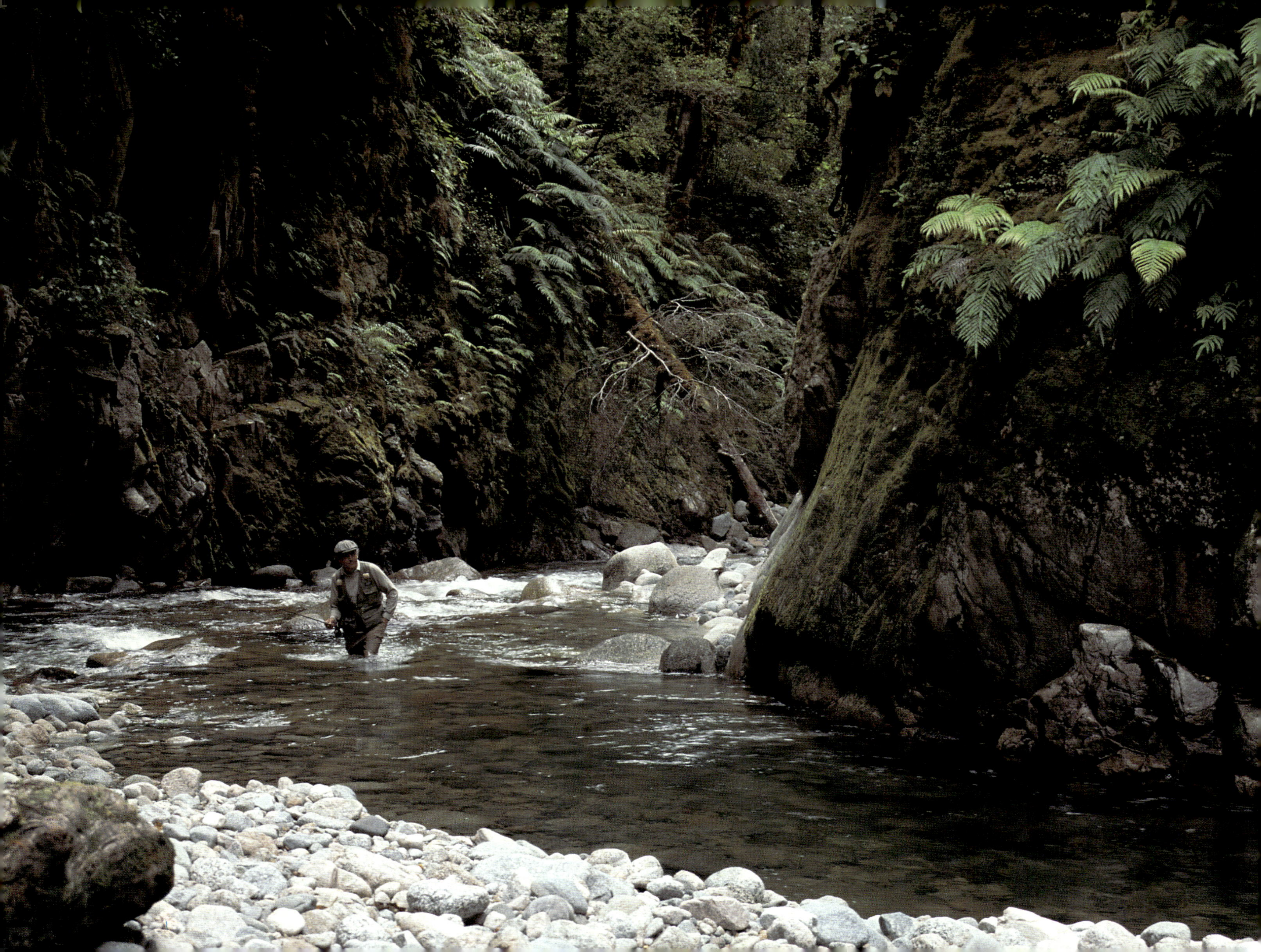

Sneaking around one more corner. The Buller River has many tributaries like this one. They all require anglers to "fish wet" because river crossings are numerous and often deep.

Paradise duck chicks. At times the paradise ducks can be a nuisance to a stalking angler as they splash their deception upstream. But our wild open spaces would be poorer without them.

Left:
A river for youthful anglers. Many southern rivers have deep gorges somewhere along their length. Merely getting to the river can be an adventure.

Soon to be released. A well-conditioned brown trout, lies on top of a net in shallow water. The release of this fish will help maintain the stream as an attractive place for other anglers and also keep healthy breeding stock present.

Images of Silver 39

wild trout, coupled with its will to survive, combine to make the trout of the South Island back country a difficult and elusive quarry.

Back in Westland the anglers advance, rods at the trail, carefully picking a route through the jumble of bankside boulders and tangled driftwood, gaze fixed firmly on the river's edge and diagonally out into the middle of the stream. While no sunlight plays on the water, conditions for sighting fish are excellent, the steep, forested slopes ensuring that little reflection or surface glare inhibits vision through the slightly coloured water column.

Too late. The lead angler starts and mutters a stifled 'Damn' as a large torpedo shape glides without great panic, but with business-like precision towards mid-stream to be swallowed up within seconds amidst the green depths of the pool. Vowing to be even more cautious, the anglers resume the search. One fish is seen, lying 'doggo' towards the middle of the stream in three or four metres of water but is ignored in favour of easier prey.

The river begins to narrow towards the head of the 100-metre long run and gradually the size of the boulders increases forming pockets up to two metres long. As the first of these is approached the lead angler stiffens, becomes as motionless as a heron as eyes search the pocket. Yes, there it is, a big trout weaving from side to side, obviously feeding on nymphs. As he watches the angler marvels at the camouflage of this beautiful, wild creature. What was it that first alerted his attention – a weaving tail, a flash of white inside a prodigious maw, or the slightly discordant green back not quite fitting the surrounding river stones? Was it the distinctive torpedo shape or the sudden revealing of a light-coloured rock as the fish moved to one side to feed? In truth any one of these may have alerted the angler. Perhaps one of them just hinted at the possibility, the merest suggestion of a fish, and one or more confirmed that suspicion. It is on such powers of observation, and the use of a sixth sense, upon which the successful back country angler must draw, just as the deer hunter very rarely sees the whole of a deer at first but is alerted to the flick of an ear, a slight movement, a colour difference or shape. It is little wonder then that proficient hunters of animals quickly adapt to become good hunters of fish.

Initially all newcomers experience difficulty with both reading the water and sighting fish before they have detected the presence of the angler. Overseas trout fishers in particular, unless they have had experience on spring creeks, such as those in some of the western U.S. states, find spotting some fish very hard. As a fishing guide I am frequently astonished by the inability of my clients to see even (to me) the most obvious of fish. Most make an attempt, especially if they come from a hunting background, and by the end of a two- or three-week trip to New Zealand have developed a reasonable degree of proficiency. Some make no effort to learn. One angler of my acquaintance spends weeks in New Zealand every year but still relies entirely on the guide not only to spot the fish for him, but also to tell him where to cast and when to strike. In effect the guide becomes his eyes. He's happy with that situation and catches his share of fish. He's a guide's delight really for he does exactly what he is told!

Meanwhile our Westland anglers are enjoying success, picking a pocket or two and tempting the resident trout with appropriate patterns. A skilled back country angler searches carefully in front of obstructions too. Westland rivers are full of large boulders, flood-borne logs and even dead standing trees, testimony to the immense forces of flood and earthquake which are constantly remoulding the untamed landscape. A study of water hydraulics indicates that a body of water rushing towards an obstruction creates a zone of slower moving water for some distance in front of it. In much the way that ship designers have discovered that a bulbous bow is more efficient than a sharply pointed one, trout have adapted to the niche in front of rather than directly behind an obstruction. The uninitiated will often walk right past or spook a trout in such a place.

The eye of the pool is worth careful scrutiny. While not always easy to fish because of back eddies and a current which changes direction suddenly, trout are frequently to be found there because of the abundance of food being sluiced through the narrowest part of the pool. Under the jumble of white water where one pool or run issues into another is frequently the home of the largest fish in the vicinity.

Few Westland rivers are easily negotiated, and if one is forced by the strength and depth of the current to stay on one bank, frequent detours into the forest are necessary. While making such a detour our anglers obtain a bird's-eye view of a deep, green pool of prodigious depth.

More challenging waters on The Coast. Places like this hold few trout. Quantity is replaced by quality.

Below:
In the McKenzie country. Dozens of fine streams like this one cross the McKenzie country of inland Canterbury. Both brown and rainbow trout are to be found.

Right:
Angler and spectator. Tim Varley and the distant angler both focussed on one thing ahead – an enticing, rising trout.

A battle high in the Inangahua River. At times great distances may separate the pools of The Inangahua. The trout are few. A place for the angler who appreciates the environment as much as catching fish.

Images of Silver 43

From an elevated position a number of trout of mouth-watering proportions are feeding avidly, hovering under floating morsels and breaking the surface with a casualness born of the conceit that comes with a sense of total security, safe in the knowledge that they are untouchable in such a situation. It is no accident that the largest fish are normally found in the biggest pools. Unless one is lucky enough to strike a time when the fish are approachable and feeding, such trout have few serious predators. The deep pools are little affected by even the most dramatic of flood events, providing sanctuary and safety until the flood waters recede. But today there is nothing to be done but watch in awe and admiration as the ladies and gentlemen of the river disport themselves.

Despite great vigilance, more fish are spooked from seemingly impossibly shallow margins. A characteristic of browns especially, is to hold in very shallow water following a fresh in the river. While the water may be shallow it is not always easy to see the fish, especially if that part of the river is lying in deep shade and the rest is in the sun, or if the river stones have assumed a coating of dark algae. The adage, 'fish the edges first' certainly applies here. But while fish may be clearly seen to be feeding in shallow water they are not always easy to take with an artificial fly. Any disturbance caused by the fly contacting the water, or the leader cutting the surface like a knife, may be sufficient to alarm a fish feeding nervously in a relatively vulnerable situation.

Perhaps the most difficult part of the river in which to spot fish, and one which is most likely to be occupied by rainbows where the two species co-exist, is the fast, mid-stream water of moderate depth where the fish are protected by a broken, tumbled surface and varied stream bed topography. As fishing pressure intensifies more and more fish will occupy this niche, and the ability to spot fish there will often constitute the difference between a poor day and a highly successful one. The trick is to see beneath the confused surface by using 'windows' or patches of relatively smooth water. The experienced fish spotter fixes the gaze upon one of these before it reaches the zone being explored. Sometimes minutes of watching will produce but a fleeting glimpse of what could be a fish, but sufficient to pinpoint a spot worth fishing to with a large dry fly or nymph and indicator.

Sighting fish is always hard in these places, but doubly so on a windy, grey day or on a day when the sun is partially obscured by passing cloud. It is extremely difficult to re-focus in conditions of changing light. I prefer bright, sunny conditions with little or no wind. A gentle upstream breeze is fine. As all who have fished in our high rainfall back country areas will attest, such conditions are relatively rare, and occur on perhaps 25 per cent of days, or less in some seasons. Seasonal variations occur. Very early and late in the season I'd rather have a sky of high overcast or even heavy cloud or fog than bright sunlight because the low angle of the sun tends to cast a shadow on one side of the valley in early spring and autumn, making fish spotting difficult and even impossible at times.

Indeed, some of the finest back country fishing I have ever experienced was on a gloomy Westland day when the rain came down in buckets. As the river rose several centimetres the fish took advantage of the extra food on offer and fed avidly on or near the surface. At one point a pool which I'd often found difficult in normal conditions came alive as the usually cagey trout fed with gay abandon, taking without hesitation almost anything on offer.

The days immediately following a major flood can produce astounding fishing. Unable to hold in the turbulent mid-stream current, browns especially come to the edges to feed in sheltered pockets. If the water is still somewhat discoloured so much the better as the fish lose a lot of their caution.

There are times though when fish are plainly visible to even the untrained eye but are sluggish and disinterested in food. I know one such pool on the Karamea River of North West Nelson. Trout are nearly always found there in abundance, usually lying towards the tail or close in on the edges. For some unaccountable reason they rarely feed during daylight hours, ignoring most offerings but sporadically and only half-heartedly taking a natural. A closer look at these fish, if one is lucky enough to catch one, indicates that some of them are in decline; older, dark-coloured fish past their silvery peak. Many are hook-jawed jacks with outsize heads and vicious teeth. While not in poor condition they are not in their prime either, and may just be using this long, slow-flowing pool as a geriatric hospital of sorts. But they are certainly easy to see, and a good place to introduce

Almost bank to bank. The angler has to wade from his bank opposite in pursuit of a strong backcountry brown seeking the near shore.

46 Images of Silver

Eluding the net. Fiordland streambeds like this one were carved deep by glacial action. The remaining pools harbour elusive, cruising trout.

somebody new to the back country scene, by whetting the appetite with promises of things to come in the pools around the bend where the fish are fit, but perfectly camouflaged.

Our Westland anglers have had a good day, spotting 20 or 30 fish all told and landing half a dozen between them, ranging up to 3kg or so. By our standards this is a good day's fishing with the modest numbers being more than compensated for by the size of the fish, their fighting ability and the sheer natural beauty of the place in which they reside.

The relative paucity of trout in many of our back country streams poses problems for anglers in less than perfect conditions, which, in fact, exist most of the time. First-time visitors to a river, unaccompanied by one familiar with the area are indeed 'up against it'. One develops a high degree of familiarity with a water which is frequently visited, and while surprises are always likely it is possible to isolate the best fish-holding water, or perhaps more to the point, water which is likely to provide fish accessible to the angler. While it is wonderful to watch and admire fish feeding in impossible-to-reach situations we would be deluding ourselves if we didn't admit to a desire to find some which are catchable. This being the case then, one eliminates quite considerable parts of most back country rivers from contention immediately. While the experienced angler does this unconsciously, it can also be practised by a total newcomer, with a fair degree of confidence. Large trout require ready access to both food and sanctuary. If this elementary principle is kept firmly in mind it will assist the stalking process immeasurably.

There is little doubt that trout are easier to fool and catch in fast water. Not only does the disturbed water surface break up the outline of the hunter; it also provides the current carrying the food to the fish without the fish having to expend great energy actively searching out its prey. As a general rule then, trout will be easier to catch in faster, broken water with numerous depressions, large rocks, jutting bank extensions and the like than they will be in the smooth glide at the tail of a pool or on a wide, slow-flowing, featureless run no matter how picturesque it may look with the nearby towering mountains reflected upon its glassy surface. Similarly, stream junctions should be approached cautiously no

Trout in sight. The angler leans forward just a little hoping for more reach, tense, expectant but not yet successful.

matter how tiny the tributary. Such places appear to possess a magnetic attraction for trout. Perhaps it is the promise of extra food, or slightly warmer or cooler water temperatures, but such places are true hot spots.

Large, deep pools provide trout with the sanctuary they so often desire, but often make them unattainable. Exceptions do occur, and few sights are designed to raise pulse rates and blood pressure more than big fish taking readily from the surface. If set in feeding mode such fish are the stuff of dreams. Too often though, the hulking pool residents are inclined to lie impossibly deep, tempting but out of reach to normal mortals. No, it is often more productive to move on to the boulder-studded run around the corner.

Only rarely do fish hold in the very fast white water such as the rapid between pools, but before writing off such a place altogether examine it carefully. Look for any possible holding water in front of or behind rocks, in a slight depression or right at the top of the rapid just as it begins its headlong plunge into the next pool. We sometimes receive pleasant surprises, especially fishing such places blind at times of very low flow in the height of summer. Fishing pressure and the need to find highly oxygenated water sometimes induces fish to seek such seemingly inauspicious and inhospitable niches.

Perhaps the key to successful back country angling, even on totally unfamiliar water is to fish with a companion. Even on the brightest of summer days it is frequently possible to spot fish by sighting them from elevated positions. If one of the party is able to remain concealed by low scrub, bush or behind riverside boulders, a great advantage lies with the angler. We frequently fish in such a way, guiding the other angler onto fish which are impossible to see at river level until it is too late and the fish has spooked. In very broken water I will often find a convenient rock even in mid-stream to perch upon, gambling that the turbulent surface will preclude detection. On wider rivers I often utilise the large boulders for this purpose with quite remarkable results.

As mentioned earlier, grey, overcast, foggy and even heavy rain days need not lessen the expectations of good sport. Indeed, such conditions can enhance it. A truly stealthy stalk in promising water will often enable one to approach to within a few metres of a fish undetected. From close proximity one angler can direct the other or, back slowly off and try for it.

One of the best browns I have ever taken was caught on one of the most miserable days I have ever experienced on a Westland river. It was raining so hard as our small party left the hut that I seriously wondered about our sanity in proceeding. Donning already sodden parkas we stepped out into the full force of the rain storm, glancing wistfully at the embers of the breakfast fire. Rods were already assembled from the previous day so without delay we were swallowed up in the dense, dripping forest, three dark shapes merging into the gloom under the giant podocarps. Cutting across a narrow peninsula of forest we dropped into a dry watercourse. A few more metres and we were on the river bank. Upstream the interlocking spurs were shrouded in mist. Surprisingly, the river was still flowing normally but we knew it couldn't last with the torrents of rain descending so we hastened through the first three shallow crossings before beginning the search for fish. Eagle-eyed Les was practically invisible on the high, bush-covered terrace. As we waited patiently he methodically covered the bouldery run.

'There's one, feeding well too. Get into it, Graeme.'

Without needing any further urging I unhooked the pheasant tail nymph and stripped a few metres of line from the reel. At river level the fish was invisible, totally obscured by the great fat raindrops battering the surface. Quickly I identified the rock the fish was lying in front of, surprised that a fish would feed in such shallow water. A couple of false casts to gauge distance and then I plopped the nymph a metre above the rock according to Les's instructions. The mahogany floating line was swallowed up in the gloom but my bank-side mentor had the fish clearly in view and called 'Strike' as it clearly rolled in the water to intercept the nymph. Water boiled as the line straightened and the rod arched and the trout created a bow wave as it sped across the shallow run. 'Yipee,' shouted my fish spotter as he fumbled inside his already soaked day bag for his camera.

It was obvious that this brownie was not going to be easily subdued and it fairly raced upstream through the protruding boulders, finally taking sanctuary in a deep scoop

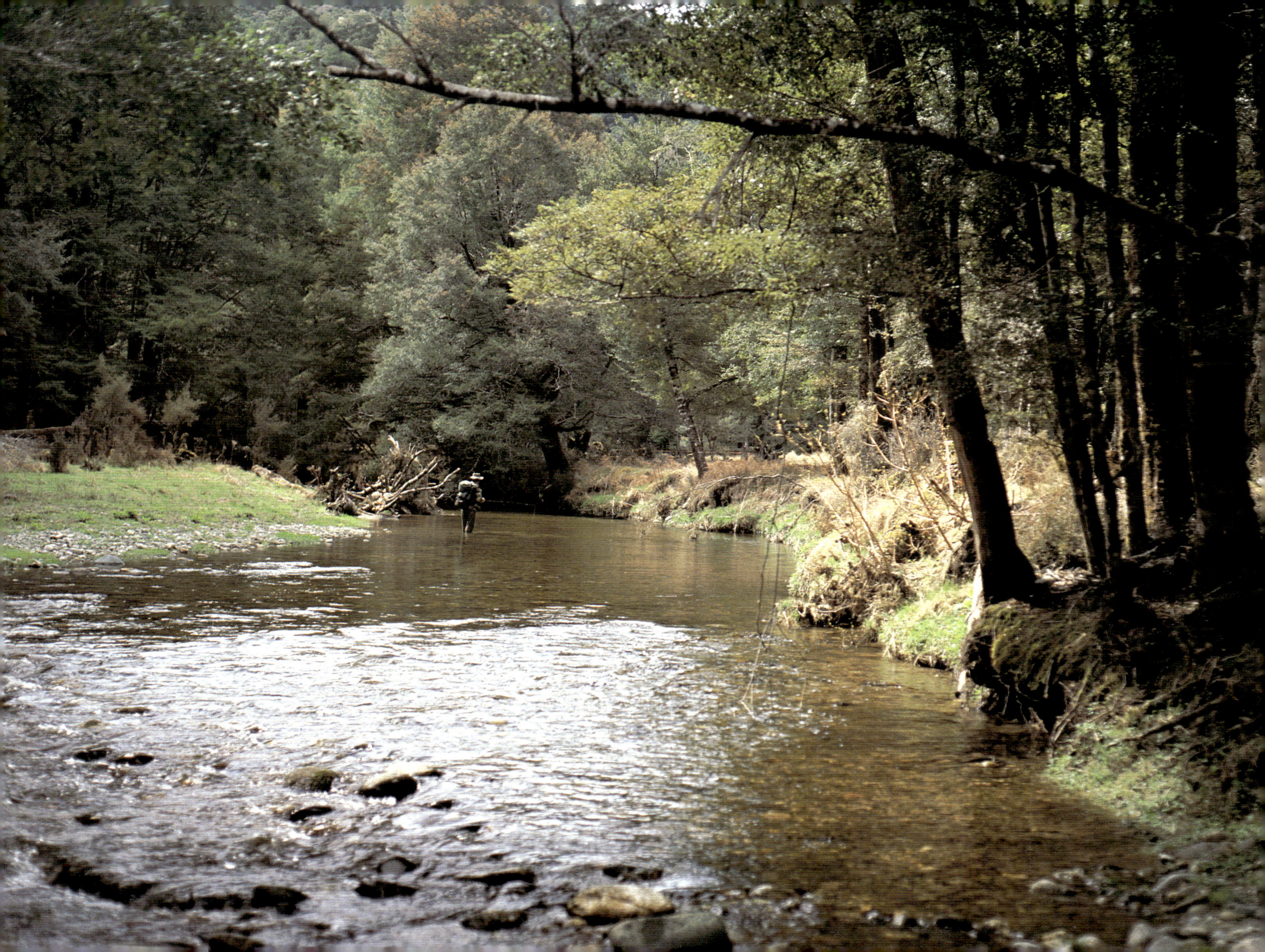

Left:
A Maruia tributary. The Maruia feeder streams are vital as spawning waters. Maintaining riverbed and bank stability must be a priority for land users and authorities.

A lofty observer. Tuis are commonly seen along many South Island bush streams.

Autumn sparkle. As the sun sinks a little lower in March rivers acquire a warm sparkle. Riverbed algal growth and riverbank flowers add colour to this pleasant time of the fishing season.

Images of Silver 53

overhung by a moss-festooned beech limb at the very top of the run. Stumbling and slipping I followed and applied heavy downstream pressure as it sulked on the bottom. Impasse. Apart from the thrumming of the current on the line and the occasional bump, angler and fish remained in stalemate for many long minutes. Eventually the steady pressure began to tell and the fish moved downstream a few metres before facing the current yet again.

Three times that happened before the final, anticipated downstream rush. This time I was stumbling downstream in hot pursuit, reeling in frantically. Part way down the run I managed to apply sidestrain and with surprising ease was able to coax the tired fish into a shallow pocket where it was easily netted. For the first time I had a good look at my prize, a superbly conditioned hen fish with green back and just a few huge red and black spots over a background of pure silver. Estimates placed the fish at around 4kg, my best from the river to this day. Despite the poor light a few hurried photos were taken and the fish returned to fight another day.

In all likelihood I'd never have managed to hook that fish alone in such extreme conditions. Despite the heavy rain it was not until early afternoon that the river showed signs of rising and we enjoyed some memorable fishing, taking turns at spotting and fishing before discretion dictated a retreat to dry clothes and a warm fire. The day had provided yet more indelible memories and testimony to the efficacy of the stalking approach.

CHAPTER FOUR
Back Country Fishing Technique

During my 'apprenticeship' as a fly fisher I spent much time on the river with a highly skilled, dedicated and innovative angler of my acquaintance. I learnt a great deal from him in terms of technique, particularly on how to fish the dry fly and nymph on the Motueka River, lessons which provided a platform from which to launch forth into the intricacies of the sport. In retrospect I realise just how good an angler my friend was, as by today's standards his equipment was relatively crude. That he caught many, many fish in the height of mid-summer using a #8 rod and line is a source of great amazement to me now, and testimony to his stalking and casting ability. I would venture to suggest that very few anglers would enjoy such success on that river today using a #8 fibreglass rod, which leads one to ponder on whether there are fewer fish to be caught or if the trout have become more wary due to increasing angler pressure. I tend to favour the latter theory.

The same may be the case on most back country rivers. For better or worse they have been 'discovered'. Some of us discovered them 20 or more years ago. The word spread quickly, and now thousands of angler days per season are put in on some river systems; small wonder that the fish are becoming more difficult to fool. It seems logical then to adopt techniques which will optimise angling opportunities.

Technique has, then, of necessity become more refined in recent times. The days of throwing virtually any pattern or size of fly at a fish have long since gone, especially when the streams reduce in volume in dry weather to a fraction of their early season spring flow. Recently a companion and I experienced a frustrating but fascinating day which exemplifies this contention.

Mid-February is normally the time of year when one can expect a high percentage of fine, sunny days in this country. While I have also experienced some incredibly wet weather at this time too, the odds are that conditions will be pleasant. But this can be a two-edged sword. Angling pressure is likely to be relatively high at this time, and as mentioned, low water, while providing good spotting conditions, makes for generally tough fishing.

That day was typical of the season. Low water made for easy river crossings, enabling

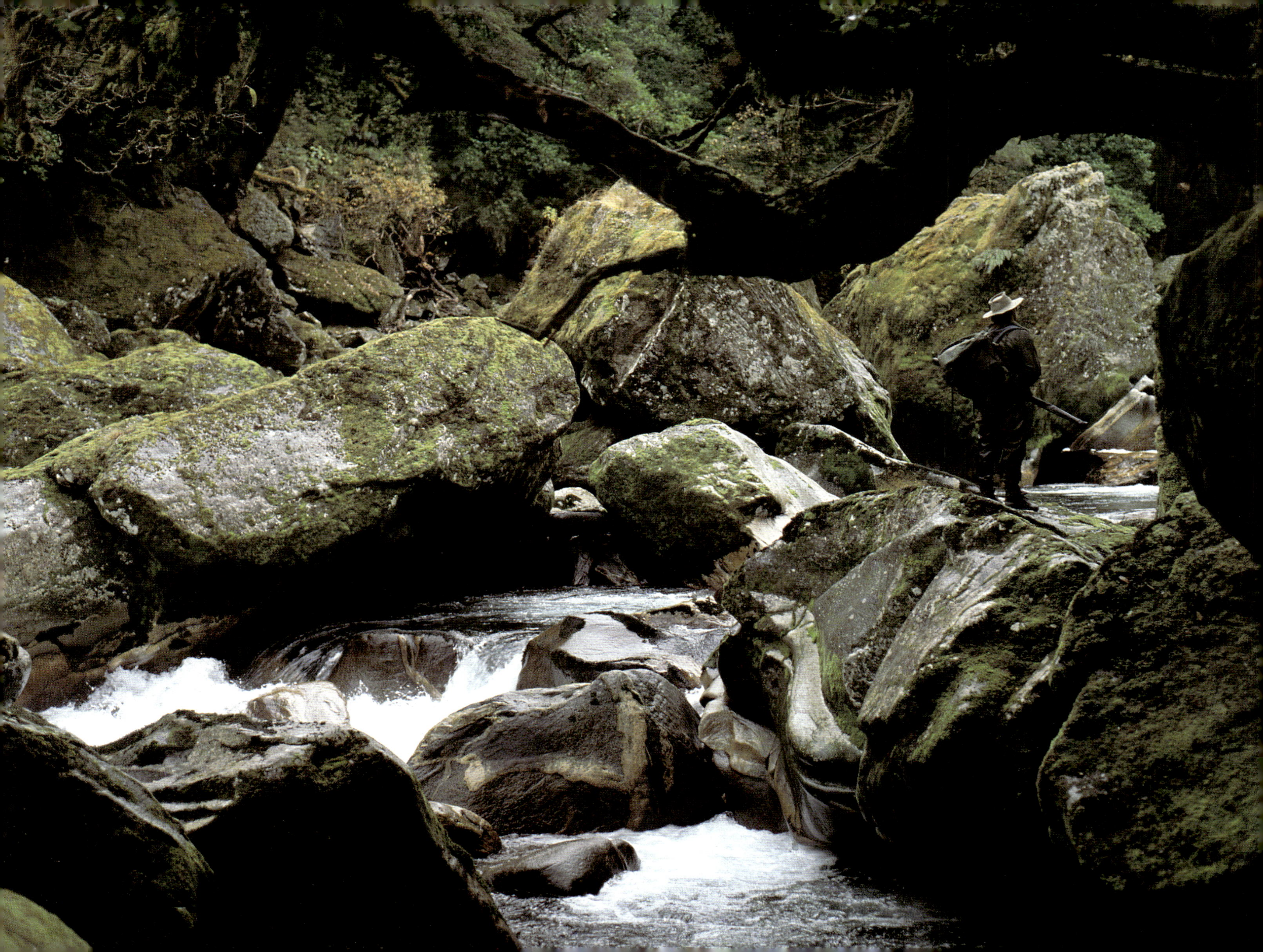

Just off the Milford track – Clinton River. Past glacial action in the Clinton valley dropped a series of boulder dams – obstacles to anglers and trout.

Successful fly patterns. A sedge fly can sometimes rise those fussy, selective feeders. Probably the most widely used nymph pattern in the South Island high country – Hare and Copper Nymph.

An anglers' delight. Two very large trout cruise upstream in a deep pool. With both banks steep and bush clad and the water several metres deep these fish remain quite safe.

Images of Silver 57

much more water to be fished than normal. The sun beat down from a near cloudless sky and the distant, snow grass-clothed mountains shimmered in the heat haze. Glancing upstream we saw the river bouncing happily through a seemingly patternless, disordered jumble of large, grey rocks. Really, conditions were perfect and I was confident of a good day. My companion, Tom, had proved his ability to outwit a goodly number of fish using nymphs blind on a river meandering through manicured fields, and was keen to try his skill on the wilder, back country water.

Things didn't work out as planned. The first four hours drew a total blank. Oh, we saw fish all right, plenty of them, and in feeding mode too, but hooking them was another story. The trout appeared to be concentrated largely in long, relatively calm runs and in the large, deep pools so typical of the river. The pattern soon became clear. As soon as the fly alighted on the surface the fish spooked, possibly. I surmised, because of the line shadow, so painfully obvious as it cut the surface like a knife. After we had both had our egos badly damaged it was a case of 'back to the drawing board'.

Clearly, a change of approach was the only way to save the day, so we deliberately walked past the long glides and turquoise pools. We waded the river to an area of broken water that I would not normally have bothered with because the entire river sliced through a narrow, near-staircase rapid, creating a maelstrom of white water much appreciated by the rafters. This day the rapid was a tame shadow of its normal self. Quite distinct, albeit small, pockets formed between the massive, rounded boulders, and towards the top of the 'run', for that is what it had become, a significant stretch of relatively calm water had appeared.

In the previous days success had been enjoyed using much smaller than usual patterns so perhaps they would work there too. The first few pockets appeared to have no residents, but a large, dark shape methodically working the third quickened the pulse. Dispensing with the large dry fly adorning Tom's leader I hastily tied on a #18, weighted pheasant tail nymph and rolled a tiny cigar of soft lead onto the tippet 30 centimetres from the point. A scrap of orange glo-bug yarn was attached above a leader knot a metre and a half from the nymph and sprayed with fly floatant. A well-aimed cast lobbed the nymph up into the fast water a metre or so above the fish.

I didn't see the fish take but the indicator left no doubt whatsoever as it was dragged savagely under the surface. 'Strike', I yelled, but needlessly as Tom was equal to the situation and hit the fish hard, producing an almost simultaneous thrashing leap sideways. Three times that beautiful fish slapped down onto the water surface, each leap taking it further towards the middle of the river and the swift, white water racing through the narrow gap. It sulked briefly behind a boulder on the far side but soon succumbed to the strength of the current and tried to use it to effect an escape, but the large, deep pool at the bottom of the run was in the angler's favour. Within five minutes a fine fish was brought flapping to the gently sloping sandy shore where I was able to remove the tiny nymph without fuss. The photo of the 3kg trout graces the wall of my study, the smile on the face of my companion testimony to his delight.

Two more fell victim to the tiny nymph in that wild run. Each was landed on the sandy beach of the handy pool. The change of tactics had worked. One more fish was landed that day, taken on a dry fly fished blind through a shallow, broken run. Again, a small pattern was the answer. This time we used a #16 parachute adams, a special favourite because of its visibility in joggly water.

There is a myth abroad in some quarters that large back country trout will take only large flies. Not so. I have proved to my complete satisfaction that small patterns frequently succeed over large ones, especially when the fish are edgy or relatively disinterested. One day late in the 1992/93 season I encountered a number of fish seemingly disinterested in food of any type. All the same I tried them with the more usual back country patterns in sizes 10 and 12 with no response at all. One fish refused to spook but would not look at my well-presented offers. With little conviction I went for my tiny weighted pheasant tail in size 18. The response was immediate. Even though the nymph clearly failed to reach the correct depth the fish moved towards it, obviously interested, but failed to intercept it. I tried again, this time with a tiny split shot on the tippet. Without the slightest hesitation

A trout under control. The Mohikanui River, shown here, is remote requiring an angler to either tramp for many hours from the road end or to meet the expense of helicopter or fixed wing.

Above:
Rimu – Red Pine (Dacrydium cupressinum). The rich forests of the back country often cloak stalking anglers. Tall rimus are among the most impressive trees particularly along the West Coast.

Raft fishing. Popular on some North Island rivers but also practised by some adventurous Southerners to reach otherwise inaccessible places.

the nymph was sucked in. As the white mouth clamped down on it I struck and the battle was on. I was eventually forced to cross the river to land and release the fish. The small pattern had worked again and continued to do so a number of times that day. I cite these examples to illustrate the importance of being prepared to adapt to changed conditions.

When the photographer and I first began fishing the now well-known streams of North West Nelson and Westland we gave little consideration to matters such as clothing and the equipment we fished with. A casual glance through a copy of Stalking Trout will attest to the fact that we wore clothing which was warm, comfortable and sandfly proof rather than designed to tone in with the forest greens. I thought nothing of carrying a red back pack and wearing a light-coloured hat. While we enjoyed remarkable angling success in those heady days when some streams were fished on only a few occasions each season, it didn't take long to realise that some fish were being spooked by the use of inappropriately coloured clothing.

While often not pictures of sartorial elegance on some of our earlier exploratory trips we always had the good sense to wear clothing which was warm and relatively waterproof. For this reason I still include items such as woollen or polypropolene vests and long-johns, woollen shirts and sweaters and a top quality rain jacket, preferably in camo or some neutral colour like deep green or brown. Nowadays, partly for appearance's sake, but also for comfort, I wear a pair of light cotton trousers in green, grey or earth colour over a pair of woollen long johns. Apart from day trips, using a helicopter for access, even stocking foot waders are a little too bulky to carry on extended trips unless the weather and water conditions are very cold. Long johns provide a fair degree of warmth, even when wet and cotton trousers dry quickly in normal summer conditions but don't drag one down excessively when wet. My main concession to modern trends is to wear a pair of felt-soled wading shoes or boots. As one who spends scores of days in the back country I can vouch for the worth of them, especially on wet, lichen-encrusted rocks. The degree of security provided on slippery rocks is nothing short of amazing.

Just recently I spent a number of days on the Buller river with some friends. Packing in haste, I left out my wading boots, a decision I was to regret after a number of tumbles into an icy, late autumn river.

Opinions vary over the use of camo clothing. I now swear by green camo in forested areas, but prefer earth colours i.e. fawn, tan and grey for wide, open river beds with little vegetation and many light-coloured boulders. A matching hat is essential. Fishing guides despair when they meet a client for the first time clad in perfectly toning jacket and trousers but who insists on wearing his 'lucky' yellow, scarlet or hot pink baseball style hat emblazoned with the name of a bone-fishing outfitter in Belize! That is a situation paralleled to a degree by rod manufacturers who insist on making rods with a bright chromium tip. But that's another story.

In recent years line manufacturers have heeded the call for dull and even dark-coloured lines. While the arguments over bright, even fluoro colours versus dull colours rage on, from where I sit it seems logical when targeting extremely wary, wild fish to avoid lines which reflect light or contrast greatly with the immediate surroundings. Regrettably, one famous line manufacturer has produced a line which is so dark that it simply cannot be seen on the water in some situations so that mending line is very difficult, especially in poor light. This company's main competitor has produced a similar line in a lighter grey which to me is perfect. I can see it, but the colour is such that it tones in well with bank side surroundings.

Another school of thought suggests, quite logically, that lines should not contrast with the light sky, and hence favours ivory, tan, buckskin or light blue. And why not? I've used all these colours successfully in even the most difficult of situations.

I'll contend that casting and presentation is much more important than line colour or even line weight. In our book *Catching Trout* I said that some back country trout are amongst the easiest of all to catch, while some are amongst the most difficult. A trout in the remotest mountain stream may be just as difficult to fool as some of its low country brethren who are targeted almost daily. An excess of false casting, heavy-handed presentation, or in some cases just the alighting of the fly upon the water is sufficient to

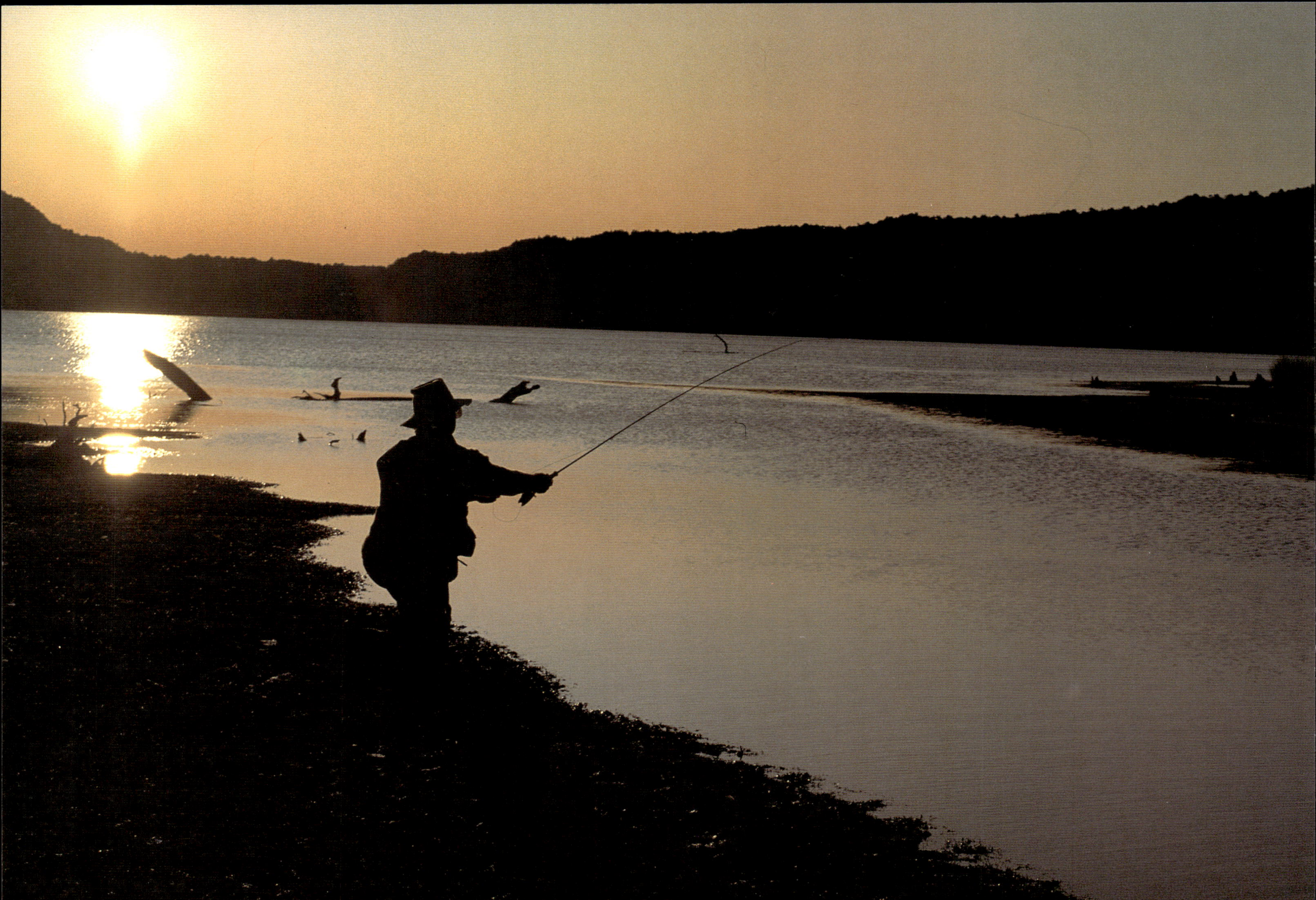

Lake Haupiri Outlet. An angler testing his luck just prior to sunset.

alert a fish residing in a smooth glide. All anglers, no matter how proficient, spook fish, and sometimes fish which appeared a formality to fool. Perhaps it is this wonderful uncertainty which draws us so inexorably.

In these 'hi-tech' days there is a wealth of superb fly fishing equipment available. One has only to glance through one of the bigger mail order catalogues to realise that the choice is nearly endless, and that the sky is the limit price-wise. While the adage 'You get what you pay for' is often true it does not necessarily always apply. A few seasons ago I had an experience which proved that point.

My client was at great pains to tell me about his new toy, a very expensive and highly regarded fly reel. En route to the river I heard a great deal about the smoothness, rugged drag system, anti-reverse features and noiseless operation. At our destination I attached the reel and threaded up the rod. Curious about the reel I stripped off some line and was surprised to find that it was in free spool mode with no drag at all, so I tightened the drag knob and started again, with exactly the same result. Somewhat perplexed I mentioned this to my companion who tested it out for himself. Removing the spool we were chagrined to discover that a miniscule spring had somehow come adrift, virtually rendering the reel useless. It was obviously a specialised job to repair, and without the correct tools it was one I was not prepared to tackle. There was nothing else for it but to resurrect the old, rather battered but functional reel that I always carry as a back-up. My client looked a trifle disgusted but said nothing and went on to have a pretty good day as I recall, while the much-vaunted but rather complex model was consigned to its suede leather bag.

I was once asked by a well-known fishing photographer what my philosophy on angling was. Without hesitation I replied KISS, or "Keep it simple stupid." Rather a trite term I know, but one I believe in implicitly all the same. I believe that anglers, like many other sportspeople, are inclined to over-complicate things. Just as a top rugby coach will sometimes insist that his players re-visit the basics of passing, catching and kicking, so I believe we should go back to basics when discussing angling. While not slavish about rod

Exhilarating fishing. This is typical of the Wangapeka River – a mixture of grassy banks and second growth native bush.

A successful strike. The upper Wangapeka River, unlike its lower reaches, flows through untouched forests. Most of the river has easy access from the Wangapeka track.

length or action I favour a rod with a medium or stiffish action of somewhere between 2.4 and 2.8 metres length, and depending on the size of stream, designed to throw a #4-6 line. If your inclinations are towards a traditional split cane rod, fine, if you can handle it. But for most anglers graphite is the only way to go. Not only is graphite forgiving in terms of the range of line weights it will handle but it also enables a relatively inexperienced angler to achieve reasonable results without too much effort.

There are some myths about back country angling which need exposing. One is that any intending angler must be capable of throwing a line a proverbial 'country mile' and to be able to land a fly on a matchbox at 20 metres. Not so. Distance casting is rarely a prerequisite to success. The ability to cast reasonably accurately is. If there is one aspect which should be concentrated on and practised at every opportunity it is casting to land a fly gently and reasonably closely to a predetermined target. In our book *Catching Trout* we stress the importance of the first cast. While it is frequently necessary to false cast to judge the amount of line needed, that needs to be achieved, preferably without placing that line over the fish. While false casting will not often bother a fish in broken or discoloured water it certainly will where the surface is smooth and the water very clear.

Perhaps the best caster I have ever seen in action, and one whose style is eminently suited to South Island back country waters is Finn, Juha Vainio. Juha, a member of the Finnish team here in New Zealand for the World Fly Fishing Championships in 1991, and well known in his own country where he frequently lectures to angling clubs, has the ability to cover a feeding fish by lifting fly line off the water and depositing the fly in just the desired spot in one, seemingly effortless motion. I observed him in action one day on a river in North West Nelson at a time when the fishing was very hard due to a period of low water and fairly intense angling pressure. He acquitted himself well under the circumstances, in situations where less accomplished casters would have drawn a blank. The secret lay in his ability to measure line intuitively without the need of false casts. The first hint that the fish had of the existence of the angler was when it felt the hook.

Balanced gear is essential for optimum performance. All too often I feel that anglers neglect their terminal tackle, i.e. leader and tippet. While not slavish about weight forward lines as opposed to double taper, for situations requiring very delicate presentation the latter are undoubtedly superior. The rub though is that less accomplished casters find it somewhat more difficult to turn over the leader with double taper lines. Balanced, carefully constructed leaders are the secret of good presentation. It is so easy to blame one's casting for an inability to turn a leader over, and while this may contribute to the problem the make-up of the leader should be suspected too. A butt section of stiff, heavy monofilament is essential. If the first two-thirds of the leader form a natural extension of the fly line there should be few difficulties in laying out the rest of the leader unless a strong downstream wind is blowing.

Invariably back country streams are rugged in nature, full of rocks and other obstructions. Without the luxury of room to play a fish unhindered break-offs are inevitable, necessitating the use of tippets of reasonable strength. In many streams the absolute minimum would be 4x, and in many situations this would need to be upped to 3x or even 2x. In 1992 I watched a companion lose eight fish out of ten hooked for the day. Every fish broke him because of his insistence on the use of 5x tippets. With the fish ranging from 2kg up to an estimated 4kg I would have preferred to take my chances of spooking fish with heavier tippets than lose fish after fish after sometimes lengthy battles which left the trout exhausted and susceptible to predators.

Many of our mountain gems take the form of short, swift torrents, interspersed, where the rushing waters take a brief rest, by short, often very deep pools. While some fish – usually, younger, smaller fish – will be found in pockets between pools, the stalking angler targets the bigger holding water. Such streams, typical of the very headwater fisheries, have little in the way of runs or even significant pockets. In their haste many anglers fish these pools poorly. In some streams each major pool holds one or more large trout, but there is often only one good opportunity to hook and land one of them. If the tail end fish is spooked it is almost certain to rush upstream and alarm others.

Similarly, a hooked fish is very likely to alert others with its struggles. If there is one

Right: *The Leslie River – northwest Nelson. A river which could benefit from catch and release only. A beautiful place worthy of preservation.*

Riverbed texture. With high country trout having such good visibility from pristine streams it is important for an angler to blend with his surrounds as well as possible.

Left:
A riverside lunch. The finest cup of tea one can taste is one prepared on an open fire with the water touched by woodsmoke.

70 Images of Silver

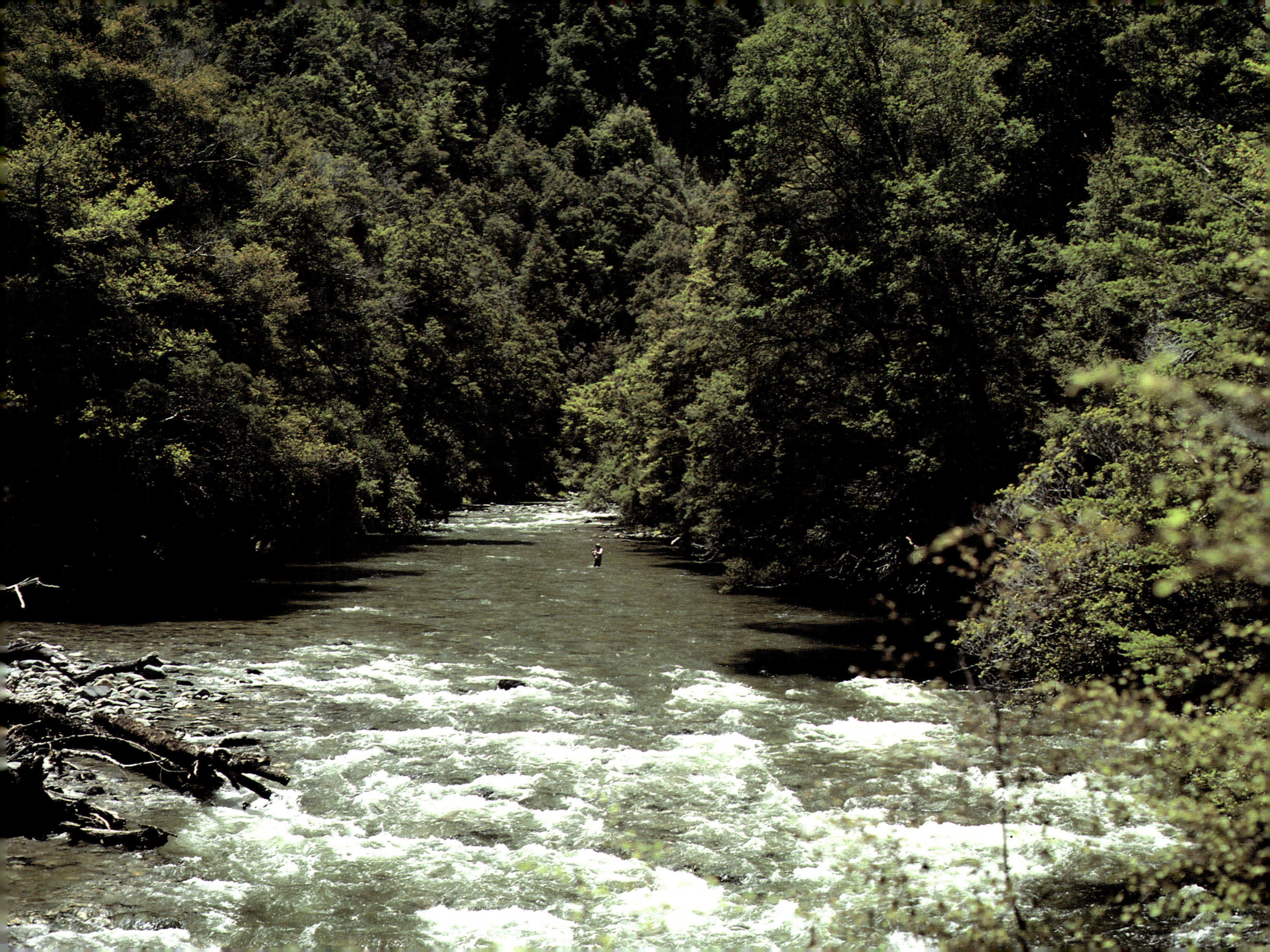

niche where the ultimate in caution is necessary it is that one. The tendency is to approach both too quickly and to move too far up the pool. The prudent angler stands well back and observes carefully.

Heeding my own advice recently resulted in a notable hook-up. I was on the Wangapeka, that well-stocked but frustratingly difficult stream, the main tributary of the Motueka. The day was one typical of that fine river. I'd seen many superb trout but as usual all had eluded me. This pool was a beauty, overhung by an elegant, broadly spread beech tree adjacent to the track on which I crouched. There the full force of the river smashed into a large lichen-encrusted boulder. Three or four metres down in the translucent blue water a veritable giant of a trout lay nearly motionless moving almost imperceptibly to hold position. This had been the pattern for the day, and I viewed the leviathan with little excitement. From past experience I knew that such fish were quite unattainable.

Moving only my eyes I methodically covered the remainder of the pool from turbulent throat to the abruptly shallowing tail. Apart from a couple of 20 centimetre youngsters dashing hither and yon, the pool was bereft of a catchable fish. Still, I maintained station for a few minutes longer. Finally deciding to move on I stood up from the uncomfortable crouching position and turned to walk away. At just that moment I caught a glimpse of a tiny swirl right against the huge boulder a metre or so down from where the full force of the current hit. Back on alert I watched the spot like a hawk. Suddenly there it was again, a slashing rise form and then again nothing. Without further ado I changed my nymph to a #14 royal wulff and detoured away from the bank to a position well downstream. Overhanging foliage forced a cast from over the left shoulder but I was able to approach close to the fish's position without fear of alarming it.

Measuring line with a couple of false casts out to the side I lobbed the fly up into the current above the holding position. The first cast landed well wide of the desired spot but the next one was right in the feedline only centimetres from the wall of rock. Without warning the fly disappeared in a swirl and I struck instinctively. The fish was on. Who said browns don't jump? This beautiful, silver-sided creature erupted angrily from the surface three times before racing in typical Wangapeka fashion downstream, through the shallow tail and without hesitation into a swift, narrow run whereupon the barbless hook promptly fell out leaving me shaken but jubilant of my success in effecting the hook-up.

In that case, resisting the urge to move on to perceived greener pastures proved successful. The desire to move further up for a better view of a pool is almost irresistible. I know, as I still blow it by taking that one extra step forward and sending to flight every fish in the pool. If at all possible the best ploy is to view from above, especially if one is able to remain hidden.

By all accounts back country South Island brown trout behave quite differently from most others. In the famous Tongariro, for instance, browns tend to be sedentary, shy fish with mainly nocturnal feeding habits and constitute only a very small percentage of the total fish taken. The same applies in the United States. There browns search out the undercut banks, snags and rock shelves. Very rarely do they show themselves in open water, and only rarely do larger specimens readily accept dry flies. Our big browns have catholic tastes indeed. If I see a large brown feeding on or close to the surface my first attempt to hook it is with a dry fly. For me the ultimate angling experience is hooking a very large brown trout with a big dry fly. These aristocrats of the trout world frequently take such fare with heart-stopping casualness, designed to test the nerves of even the most seasoned angler. My legs still turn to jelly and my hands shake uncontrollably when confronted by a fish taking naturals in such a fashion.

That is the classic pool situation, and one which does not occur as often we would like it to. Far too often the fish are lying near the bottom or feeding on nymphs two metres down, far more difficult propositions both. But when a trout is pre-occupied with feeding from the surface it is odds on that it will take virtually any pattern offered. Matching the hatch is not as critical as it usually is on a low country river where both pattern and size are crucial. It is still important to present the fly with a minimum of disturbance but the most difficult part is timing the strike. Eagerness often overrules with

Gentle stream amid rugged country. Trout and angler strain against each other with opposite intentions. A typical Nelson stream.

Above:

Still struggling – even out of water. Ho Hill battles to hold a magnificent brown trout as he moves waterwards.

Left:

An unnamed Coleridge tributary. Vegetation overhanging both banks of the stream suggests a healthy waterway.

Images of Silver 75

disastrous results. With all the will at their command some anglers simply cannot control their impulse to strike as soon as the fish has taken the fly in. The only way to ensure a reasonable percentage of hook-ups to takes is to wait an almost interminably long time, or at least until the fish has turned down. If the rod is being held nearly parallel to the surface it is then a simple matter to strike with a firm, steady lift of the rod.

The leisurely take of a portly pool resident is not the style of those feeding in fast, bouldery runs between pools. The larger back country waters hold good numbers of fish wherever suitable feeding and holding water exists. Even if fish are not sighted in water which looks 'fishy', it is well worth prospecting with either a large, highly visible dry fly, nymph or tandem rig of a dry fly on a dropper with a nymph on the point. Favoured flies for this style of 'prospecting', often a productive and satisfying method of angling include royal wulff, the humpy and parachute adams.

Back country rivers have an ability to intimidate the new-comer. A seeming disordered jumble of boulders and flood debris has a distinct pattern to one accustomed to it, though. By breaking up the total scene into its component parts and concentrating on these a sense of order soon becomes apparent, and experience dictates the "modus operandi'.

In most situations, due to the clarity of the water and inherent wariness of the trout it is essential to stalk upstream. The upstream approach is virtually mandatory just as the use of dry fly and nymph is normally superior to lure and small wet fly. A combination of dry fly and nymph is often an excellent means of covering the water when fish are not easily spotted due to discoloured water or poor light. The method involves the use of a large, easily seen dry fly with a weighted nymph tied directly off it. Alternatively, the dry may be tied onto a short dropper. These methods are outlined in detail in our book *Catching Trout*. The dry fly acts as an excellent indicator for a take on the submerged nymph, or is quite frequently taken itself, an experience guaranteed to set the heart racing.

One problem frequently encountered in deep, fast water is that of sinking the nymph to the level of a feeding fish. An excessively large nymph often results in a spooked fish as does the use of large split shot. A method which I have employed with considerable success recently is that of using two nymphs, with a small one tied off the bend of the larger hook on a short trace of perhaps 20 centimetres. This method, which employs the weight of both nymphs to get down quickly appears to work best if the larger nymph is an easily seen attractor pattern such as one tied with krystal flash, or one of the currently popular and effective bead head nymphs. In most cases the smaller nymph, which I feel should be one representing a natural insect, is the one which is taken. The theory is that the attractor brings the smaller, more natural looking nymph to the attention of the fish.

The upstream approach to back country angling necessitates an ability to cast with reasonable accuracy and delicacy. Big trout are not easily fooled, and browns especially are easily spooked by an unnatural drift of the fly. Practice in mending line to lessen drag is an essential prerequisite for fishing for shy fish. Rarely does a back country stream with its great variety of topography flow in completely laminar fashion. Sub-surface currents too can affect the natural movement of a nymph, alerting the ever wary trout.

We have covered the subject of drag and ways of countering it to some degree in our earlier books and these are recommended for intending back country anglers. If the angler is cognisant of potential drag prior to casting some of the problems may be avoided, especially when fish are lying in difficult situations.

In summary then, back country stream technique relies on stealth. The angler is indeed a hunter. The use of appropriate clothing and equipment, including polarised glasses, is essential. In the main the approach is an upstream one and the angler will need to use long leaders and a variety of fly types, patterns, sizes and rigs to achieve success.

Just netted on a West Coast stream. This is typically West Coast. A bushclad stream – bouldery, clear, inviting. The trout – wild, lively, prized.

78 Images of Silver

A fine West Coast brown. Well known Christchurch angler Chappie Chapman proudly holds his catch before releasing it to the stream.

CHAPTER FIVE

Fishing Still Waters

I can still remember quite vividly the first trout I caught on a fly rod along the margins of a lake. From that moment a whole new and exciting facet of fishing opened before me – the magic of fishing still waters.

The fish fed, as so many do, not in the lake itself but in a deep feeder channel. It appeared to be the sole occupant of the narrow waterway, patrolling first inland away from the lake then returning along the same beat, easing sideways only to inspect for food or to take a morsel.

How different this was to a feeding river trout. This fish did not enjoy the luxury of current bringing food to it. It could not reside in one place and wait. Instead it was continually on the move actively seeking prey.

Partly through fascination but more probably to consider a way of catching the fish, I observed for some time. In about a metre and a half of water the trout continually hugged the bed never lifting high and certainly not to the surface to take flies. A nymph it appeared was the way to lure this trout.

But how should it be approached? Sheltered from any wind, the waters ahead remained unruffled, mirror-like. Any disturbance would surely alert the fish. As the trout passed me it was very close too. A waving rod would be equally alarming. It appeared that the only approach lay in 'setting a trap'. The thought was to wait until the fish fed far up the channel well out of sight then to cast a nymph. When the trout returned the line would rest as still as the water with the nymph stationary below.

More impatient now, I watched the fish swim slowly past once more, then move gradually from sight. When I considered it safe I flicked a nymph forward. The falling line sent tiny waves sideways. Then the nymph plopped and sank gradually to the bottom. With my left hand I eased as much floating line back into the weeds, leaving only the leader exposed.

The wait was short. I was still adjusting my grip on the line and concealing the rod tip when the fish nosed forward. Closer and closer it came, up to the nymph. Then, alas, past it and on towards the lake. It was then that I decided to add some life to the offering – not

A misty morning in the Nelson lakes district.

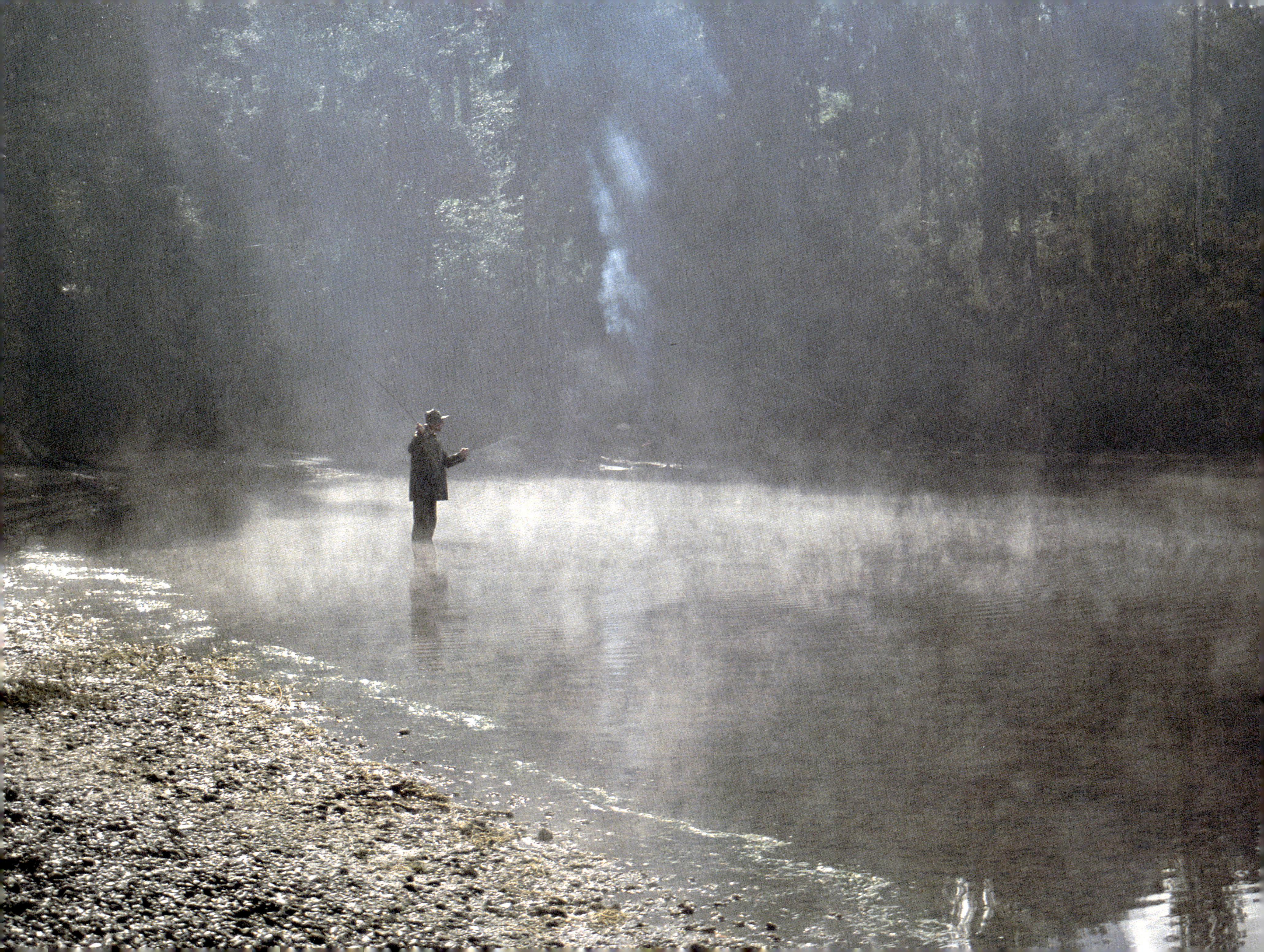

immediately but as the fish passed again.

It is not often that one has a really close and clear view of trout and intended 'bait' and particularly a side-on view. But this I enjoyed. The fish began to pass again. When it was about two metres from the nymph I tugged gently on the line. The nymph lifted quite visibly from the mud. The trout dived forwards and the immediate appearance of the white inner jaw verified its intentions. I waited until the white disappeared then struck solidly.

The rod tip lifted violently then ducked forward again as the fish responded with a desperate lunge. The immediate run, short and sharp, took the fish up the channel. But then came an immense run for the freedom of the lake. At first it bore deep, then continued in more spectacular fashion erupting from the water several times including a tail slide of several metres.

That fish took me to my backing twice before it succumbed to the net. It had earned its freedom. As expected it sped out into the lake and not up its previous feeding channel.

Since that first encounter I have repeated the act countless times but each encounter has been no less exciting, challenging or rewarding. The still water settings have been similar but each experience has retained a degree of individuality. Never have I felt a hint of indifference or of overfamiliarity.

The high country lakes of the South Island vary enormously from the very deep glacial lakes of Fiordland to tiny tussock-lined tarns all along the eastern side of the main divide. Some are unfishable along their margins except from a boat while others offer easy access right around the shore. The jade green waters in the deep south contrast markedly with the teal blue of the Mackenzie Country or the tannin brown of the West Coast.

Notable too is the variety in any one area. This is one of the lures the high country lakes have for me. Nights are often still and clear, even high in the mountains. And as the first light appears on the eastern horizon the waters on a lake ahead remain absolutely devoid of movement. When the sun first touches the water a transformation, quite sudden and spectacular, may occur – a mist forms, still at first then swirling in the gentlest of breezes. In the growing light a shape can be seen snaking across the shallows, tempting, elusive.

By mid-morning the gentle breeze may rise, now more steady and direct, from the north-west. High cirrus clouds above suggest an approaching front and hint too at the fury and foam of an angry lake later in the afternoon. But there is a hope that the front will pass quickly with a southerly change and bring stillness the following day – a stillness welcomed by a fly fisher.

Techniques used to lure trout on still waters are numerous and varied. However the focus of the text in this book is on stalking trout so the techniques suggested here relate directly to a stalking angler, mainly searching shallow lake margins.

Stalking trout must be one of the most energetic, exciting and demanding forms of fishing. It involves an angler sneaking along waterways endeavouring to remain concealed from ever-wary trout; then, once a feeding fish has been spotted, trying unobtrusively to deceive the quarry.

Stalking techniques for streams and rivers have been explained in detail – for example in *Stalking Trout*, but little has been written about stalking on still waters. While the principles remain the same, the differences in environment demand some adaptations and refinements.

The principles of stalking (stalking here being the act of finding a feeding trout without it detecting an angler's presence) relate to an angler's attire, demeanour and movement and awareness of the wariness of trout.

The use of camouflage or neutral toning clothing has been alluded to in earlier chapters and largely the principles concerning it that apply to stream fishing apply on lake edges too. However, high country lakes vary enormously in character. The differences should be considered.

At a glance most of New Zealand's native forest vegetation appears as a dull monotone of largely olive hue. But in reality and on close acquaintance, it is a wonderful

The tools of the trade. A five weight Sage rod holding a system 2 reel and six weight, double taper floating line. Ideal for stalking rivers or lake edges.

84 Images of Silver

Left:
Airborne brown – Marlborough highland lake. Much of Marlborough remains relatively dry all year. However, some fine lake and river fishing exists for the adventurous angler.

Right:
A stubborn brown. Just prior to netting the angler must be most careful, unhurried and patient.

Below:
Damselfly – lake trout diet. Hovering damselflies induce spectacular leaps from hungry, ambitious trout.

pot-pourri of greens, ranging from the soft, delicate spring growth of most beech species to the almost true olive hue of the podocarps like the elegant rimu. The angler who wears clothing which contrasts starkly with these tones does so at his or her peril.

Stalking the open, often treeless, lakes of Canterbury in mid-summer is so different from fishing in the bush country further west. One could be excused for believing that one had been transported swiftly to another land. Clothing will here need to fit in with the prevailing straw colour of the tussocks and the grey of the screes which cut swathes from the high, rocky peaks to the valleys. Earthy colours of tan, grey and khaki are more appropriate than the forest greens.

The ability of trout to detect movement is well documented. If the importance of a slow, stealthy approach is emphasised while stream fishing, it is doubly important when tackling still waters. Indeed the successful still water angler is obliged to spend much time in a stationary or near-stationary mode. This is essential not only to render the angler less visible but also to enable his or her eyes to be kept waterwards all the time.

Nature provides much cover for an angler along waterways. On even the most open of waters there is usually some natural cover which can be used to advantage. The skimpiest of thorny matagouri shrubs or clumps of snow grass or tussock are potential ambush sites. Some serious stream anglers are known to employ the aid of hunting face paint to disguise a pale face, but without going to this extreme you can use vegetation, to break up the outline of face, body or hands.

In rivers and streams feeding trout generally face upstream and often hold in one position. They often have the advantage of varying forms of obstructions for protection and the luxury of a constant flow of water bringing food as they await. Lake trout are, however, constantly on the move in search of food and often along edges with few obstructions or cover.

River trout are often protected from above too. Those hugging banks lie below overhanging vegetation or in shade. Many streams have much overhanging vegetation and huge boulders and rock shelves for fish to lie beneath. Water surfaces, rippled by constant flow often obscure the angler's visibility. Only when the wind blows are lake surfaces broken and the window to the lake bed diffused. Lake dwellers must seek the security of deep water or dive into weed beds.

For an actively stalking angler there exists a fundamental difference between still and flowing waters. He or she, when wading, should consider the affect on the waters ahead. On a lake pushing a series of waves ahead will signal the angler's presence. The same can happen on a stream but with an upstream approach it is unlikely.

In many places, because of the different nature of river and lake banks, I believe it is necessary for a lake stalker to look from a greater distance from the water's edge than a river angler.

Many lake edges, where they can be fished, are flat or gently sloping with little convenient vegetation to hide an angler. In addition the trout that cruise there frequently venture close to the shore in search of food. An angler well back from the shore may not only be less obvious but completely out of the trout's vision. This greater distance between angler and trout may appear a disadvantage when active pursuit is considered. Immediately there may be a casting problem but consideration of the territorial nature of trout and an angler's ability to predict a trout's movement can lead to a more advantageous position later. Patience and stealth are essential.

The fact that trout move up and down lake shores in reasonably predictable ways gives you a chance to spot from more elevated or other advantageous observation points. This leads to a simple adage I use along still waters – 'spot then position' – meaning: spot the trout first then position yourself to cast. Not the reverse.

Stalking along a river is largely similar but the important variation concerns the position. On a river the trout usually lies upstream and is approached from behind. On a lake a stalking angler must watch in all directions. While making your way along a shore, frequent reverse glances must be made, particularly if progress is slow as it should be. Trout

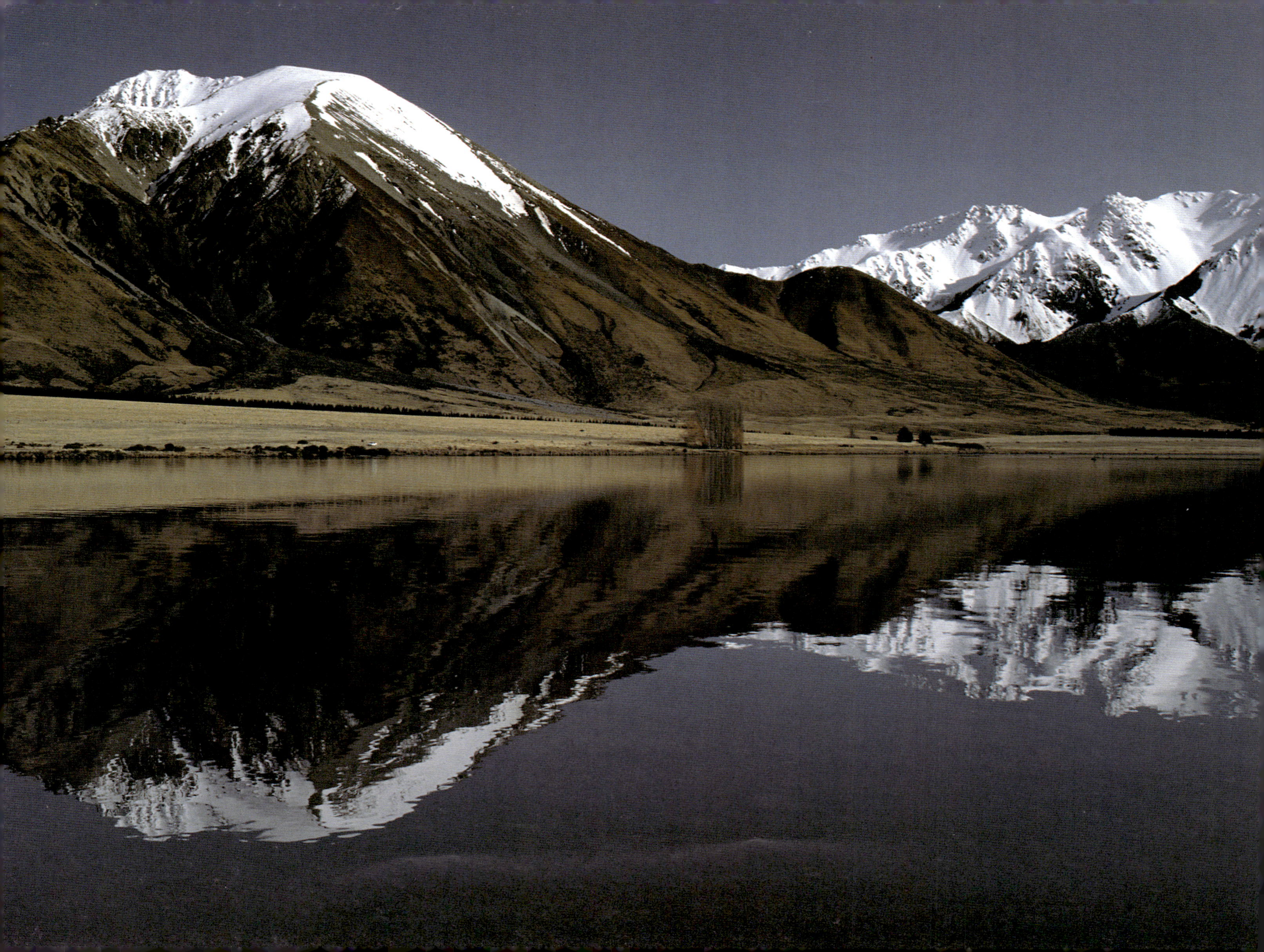

Reflections on Lake Grasmere. Like its close neighbours, Lakes Pearson and Lyndon, Grasmere provides an attractive and ever changing trout fishery.

Above:
Boating on Lake Te Anau. The southern lakes exhibit ever changing moods. One would never tire from familiarity.

Left:
Sunset over the southern lakes.

Images of Silver 89

will often move into the shallows from deep waters beyond.

Generally, on a river, the more 'ripply' the water's surface the closer an angler can get to a trout. Such water disturbance is usually due to the slope and texture of the bed. On a lake it is wind action that agitates the surface and helps to obscure an angler. Again the greater the disturbance the closer an angler can get to a fish before being detected. The reverse is also unfortunately true. Trout are more difficult to find on a wind-riffled lake. For a stalking angler closer proximity is necessary on a breezy day not only for finding trout but also for retaining contact in pursuit.

In any waterway, stream, river, lake, pond, channel, wherever – a stalking angler should expect to find trout anywhere. But there are some particular spots where trout are found more frequently and in greater numbers. Greater attention to and in these areas often adds to success.

In a lake, several areas can be isolated as 'hot spots' for trout. Probably the most important and best known is in the vicinity of an inlet stream or river. These feeder waterways provide a constant supply of food but also attract food species as well. The waters from a tributary may be a different temperature from the lake (an important factor during the hottest part of summer) while streams also attract trout at spawning times.

Lake outlets with their more stable flows and beds frequently boast the highest densities of trout populations of any waterways. Particularly at night or in the early morning, trout tend to drift back into these places to feed.

Weed beds along shallower lake margins not only provide protection for trout but are also inhabited by trout food species. Aquatic insects dwell among a multitude of obstructions as well. Hence trout are attracted to lake shores of this nature.

The security provided by the deeper waters of a lake has been mentioned earlier. Usually between the depths of a lake and shallower waters there is a steep drop-off. Along this trout will cruise. They will also venture up channels, pushing inland from a lake particularly if the inlet is reasonably deep. Well-vegetated shores attract trout because of the food source there and I've noticed, usually from a distance, that the lake side of a swamp often displays much trout activity.

These places do not encompass all the feeding niches of lakes but having a broad knowledge, as suggested here, can be of practical assistance – particularly to a stalking angler and the shallow water focus of this angling style.

Each season I try to explore a number of new waters – both rivers and lakes. Sometimes I explore places of repute, sometimes I follow intuition or even chance.

Three years ago I set out, not initially to fish a particular small lake, but to see if there were any fish there. During the last 15 minutes of a two-hour walk in from the road my pace quickened, along a broad ridge before the water below came into view. Dwarfed by 5-6,000 foot peaks behind, the lake appeared small, insignificant. Somewhat inspired and eager I was tempted to rush down to the nearest point but somehow I managed to restrain that urge and consider the prospects – albeit briefly.

An inlet stream tumbled noisily from the shore opposite. That bank could wait. Much closer lay the outlet, a deep channel flanked by swampy tussock beds on either side. If there were trout in this lake, some would reside there. I hesitated no longer. As I neared the lake level progress became more difficult. Dry tussocky slopes dropped into less inviting environs – a swarm of tiny hummocks with interlacing knee-deep channels. Not impassable, in fact ideal. My profile was kept very low while the tall vegetation concealed me almost completely. I pushed slowly on towards the lake edge and outlet channel.

Actually finding a trout in a new waterway, especially if its presence is unknown, is far more exciting to me than catching it. The first sighting immediately unfolds a host of adventures ahead – not just in the immediate future but on all visits to come.

I struggled closer then stopped just two metres from open water. I parted two tussocks that partly obscured my view ahead. While a light breeze rippled the lake surface a bright overhead sun illuminated the lake bed, allowing ideal visibility. Despite having a broad view of the mud flat ahead initially I saw nothing. Not a shape. No movement.

Disappointed, I continued to gaze ahead, eyes straining. I'm almost certain a sixth

Lake Heron in Autumn. An angler surveys the prospects ahead – a scene mixing warm autumn yellows and browns with the blue and white signalling the forthcoming winter.

A good boat – essential on the southern lakes. All of the South Island lake must be treated with caution and respect. In a very short space of time mirror like surfaces can be whipped up by a passing front.

92 Images of Silver

Watching from the bow. Southland angler, Alan Pannett, rod assembled hoping to see a telltale dimple ahead.

A tramper/angler. The only way for "the average angler" to reach many back country waters is on foot. Having tramped "in" one gains extra satisfaction.

Images of Silver 93

sense detected the fish just before I saw it. I tensed as it slid quietly past no more than a rod length away. One moment it emerged from the obscurity of the bank on my right then disappeared from view on the other side, snaking its way against tussock and reed.

Once an angler has caught the first fish of a day others seem to be easier. It's the same with spotting. As that fish moved from sight two others appeared further out, nosing along the mud. The fun I had that day lured me back to the tiny lake many times. Each time I found most of the fish in the same places – around the inlet and outlet, cruising along a distinct drop-off and among permanent weed beds.

I've found the same thing on other lakes. The most productive spots consistently provide the best sport and generally possess one or several of the features outlined earlier.

The techniques outlined below probably account for only a small percentage of the lake catch in New Zealand. They relate only to the stalking technique for an angler who has a fish in view and is in active pursuit. However, while the percentage catch may be small, the pleasure, excitement and gratification are great.

Dry fly On most occasions even the gentlest and most accurate of fly casters has difficulty landing a fly right in front of a still water trout without alarming the fish. It can be done, it is often done, but aiming a fly directly ahead of a trout is not the most highly recommended approach – especially on very calm waters.

Remembering that a fish being sought is either in view or its territorial path has been carefully observed, a dry fly angler is usually better advised to cast well ahead of the fish – say three to four metres in front (not from behind as this places the line over the fish) – or directly on what has been deemed to be the trout's feeding line. Then it is simply a matter of waiting. If the trout passes under the fly without taking, wait until it is well clear before removing the fly from the water.

This is time to try a new pattern. If a second pattern is likewise refused a tiny twitch of the fly, inducing a very small movement, may increase interest when the trout passes later.

Two patterns I like using, particularly in summer, are the green beetle and the blowfly.

Dry fly with nymph In this technique I generally use a small, slow-sinking nymph tied about a metre beyond the dry fly. Then I use one of two approaches:

First, I will endeavour to cast the fly so that it lands just within the trout's sight (say 2-3 metres ahead). The approaching trout will then detect the fly landing but also encounter a sinking and moving nymph. Alternatively, I will fish with a stationary fly along with an imitation of a nymph that will normally be found lying in or close to the surface film e.g. a midge larva pattern. The use of the dry fly here is twofold – it may be taken itself or it may indicate accurately where the tiny nymph rests so that a take can be seen.

Dry fly with dry fly On a breezy or dull day it may be very difficult to see a tiny dry fly. But often it's a minute surface fly that is preferred by a wary trout. To overcome the visibility problem I use two dry flies tied about a metre apart. The more distant fly is the smaller with the nearer one being a more visible pattern.

Nymph trap A nymph trap involves placing a nymph on a lake bed on an expected feeding line. This is done when a previously observed trout is out of sight. When the fish approaches where the nymph lies (when it is about a metre to a metre and a half away) tug the nymph gently off the bed. I've been far more successful using just one gentle tug – not more. This technique is most suitable for a pattern like the water boatman.

Nymph retrieve Nymphs like dragonfly larva imitations are most effective with this method. The technique requires the angler to cast, then allow the nymph to sink right to the lake bottom. Then the nymph is retrieved slowly at the appropriate moment.

Nymph drop As when casting a dry fly into a trout's cone of vision dropping a nymph there requires considerable skill, care and luck. Generally a small, very lightly

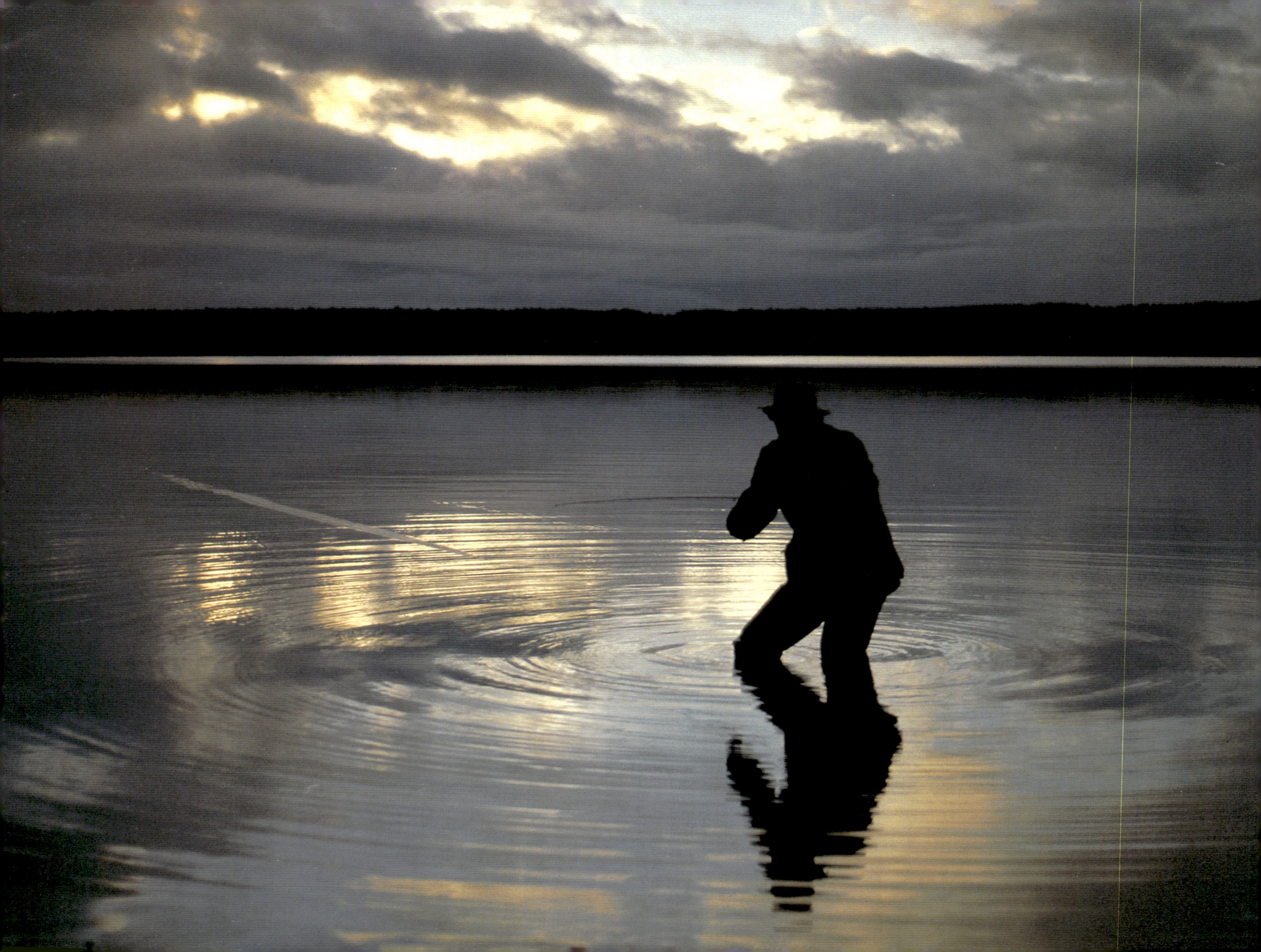

Last light on Lake Hochstetter. Hochstetter is one of many tea-coloured West Coast lakes. While these lakes do not boast great fishing reputations they are nonetheless attractive places to visit. There are trout there to be caught.

weighted nymph should be used – one that will sink only gradually. I cast a nymph in this way, without a dry fly, when the take will be clearly seen.

Lure retrieve Many anglers use this method or variations of it almost exclusively in their lake fishing. Mostly it is used in what I would call blind casting. This means that the angler casts the lure across a stream mouth, an outlet or other likely place in the hope that a fish cruises there.

For a stalking angler, however, the lure is cast into the path of a sighted trout then retrieved slowly. I prefer to drop the lure just beyond the fish's vision, thus avoiding possible alarm from the splash. This also allows a short time for the lure to sink a little before the retrieve.

I've had more success catching rainbows than browns this way. My preferred patterns are Mrs Simpson and a plain olive green lure.

The lure of the lake So often I hear it said, 'I'm a stream fisherman,' or 'He's a lake fisherman.' And I think it is largely true that most anglers do prefer to adhere to one style of fishing almost exclusively. However, my tastes are more catholic. Streams hold their fascinations – pocket water, ripply runs, deep, rock-bound pools and so on – but lakes have a lure of their own, for me an irresistible one.

There's one little lake I visit maybe twice each season. One shore is lined thick with bullrushes but the opposite bank remains more open, more accessible. The best time to visit is following a southerly change when the skies have cleared and the breeze has dropped to a whisper. Such days reveal a fascinating pattern on this little lake.

If the breeze blows, the waters ahead remain devoid of life. No insects. No birds. No trout. Yet as quickly as the breeze may spring up it can die. In the immediate stillness, across the entire glassy surface, tiny insects appear in swarms. Trout dimple the surface and occasionally, close to the rushes, jump high in the air in pursuit of hovering damsel flies. Fleet-winged birds join the foray, diving from nearby rocky outcrops and swooping low

A stance of anticipation. A lake edge cruiser lurks close. The angler is poised to strike.

A final admiring look. The trout numbers in many Canterbury and Marlborough lakes are not large. Quality trout like this should be returned to maintain breeding stock.

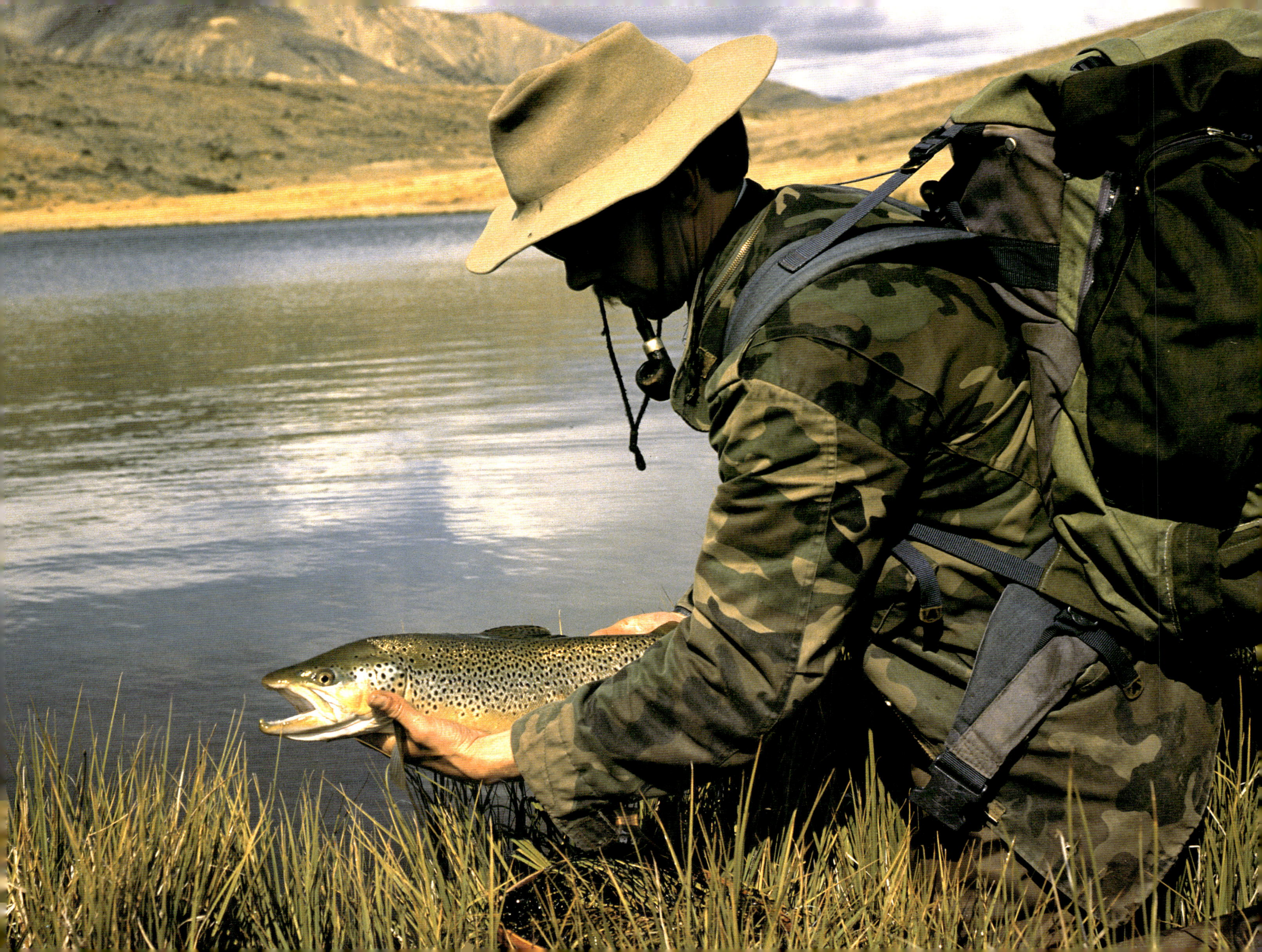

over the waters.

Then the spell may break again. Fifteen minutes of ripple. Zephyrs maybe but enough to tame the activity, quell the life. However, anticipation remains high with the knowledge that as soon as stillness returns so will the waiting life.

There's another lake I visit just once per year, deep in the heart of Fiordland. The tall, steep glacial surrounds are nothing less than majestic. The fishing is unique and I'd visit more often if time permitted.

I go there early each winter, not because that's when the fishing is best but because that's when my holidays fall. Winter days are short in Fiordland and the sun stays low in the deep glacial valleys. It may peak into the valley floors for no more than an hour early in the afternoon. That can be a fascinating time on the lake edge.

Trout, previously hidden by shadow, are revealed cruising the shallows as soon as the sun lifts from lofty summits. Amid tumbled trunks, deposited during earlier floods, they forage with tails and fins cleaving the water surface. While it provides a spotlight on the fish the sun transforms the lake in other ways too. Steam may rise from exposed mudflats and sand alike and the meeting of cool, glacial waters and warm rays produce an immediate mist, eerie, mysterious in the winter stillness. The tranquillity may prevail all day. Calm too remain the game birds – paradise ducks, greys, mallards, Canada Geese – drifting gracefully offshore, safe from hunters.

If you like catching a lot of fish this is not the place to be. But if you want a fantastic place for stalking I can think of none better. Every year it's different. Every minute something new unfolds.

Lake Heron is another place I'm lured to. Four photos that appear in this book may reveal why. They show I hope, the changeability of our lakelands.

And therein lies the lure. Mediocre fishing one moment may be great the next. Tranquillity may become storm. Around every bay, beyond every shore, a surprise. Every day, every hour, every minute fishing on still waters is an adventure.

CHAPTER SIX

Conservation and Preservation

There is little doubt that the South Island back country fisheries, which have been presented so graphically in this book through the lens of Les Hill's camera, are very special. If New Zealanders ever doubt the truth of that statement, they need only speak to a few of the ever-increasing band of visiting anglers who go to great expense and a good deal of trouble to seek them out. While the frustrations of our sometimes diabolical weather and difficult access militate against them, few who visit our wild places in search of the truly 'blue-blooded' trout which reside there come away in some way untouched by the experience.

At some stage in all serious trout angler's lives there comes a time when the actual catching of fish ceases to form their total raison d'etre. It is possible to have an outstanding day's fishing without hooking or landing a solitary one. While some may scoff at this contention I firmly believe it to be so. When one can accept and acknowledge this honestly to oneself, one has at last come of age.

Being defeated by the trout of our back country is no disgrace or cause for despondency. Other joys and rewards are there for the taking. While I would not entirely agree with Arnold Gingrich's contention that reading about fishing is actually better than the act of doing it, there is some merit in the suggestion.

Though not rich in wildlife in the form of mammals, apart from relatively low numbers of deer, goats and wild pigs, New Zealand is a bird lover's paradise. Many unique species abound in both forested and open areas and, along with numerous introduced species, they frequently fill the air with song. I never tire of the melodious notes of the native bellbird and tui as the sun brings life and light to the beech and podocarp forests. Nothing could be so perfectly designed to fit into the crisp, cool of a montane valley as the early morning mists curl smoke-like from the beckoning river.

Other avian delights may include the tame but rare blue duck or whio, the red-headed kakariki, the mournful-sounding paradise ducks or the harsh-voiced but beautiful forest-dwelling kaka.

The lake angler will encounter the ever-patrolling harrier hawk, the comical mountain parrot, the kea, and a wide range of wading birds. They may be joined by the magnificent

White heron. The white heron breeds in a colony at Okarito in south Westland. For most of the year though they feed on small fish all over the South Island. This one explores the shallows of Lake Brunner.

Streamside growth. In shady, sheltered places a host of colourful fungi may be found.

A high country hut in the Harper valley. Many such dwellings exist in the high country – welcome havens for many anglers.

Blue ducks. Often sighted by anglers as these beautiful birds feed, like trout, on nymphs in a stream. Their whistling call is often heard before the bird is seen.

Images of Silver 103

Canada goose or the shy mallard and the native grey ducks.

New Zealand's forests are unique and have evolved in the absence of browsing animals. The beech, represented by a number of types, is found practically everywhere, apart from on part of the West Coast. Typically, forests are dense, mixed and evergreen, varying but little from season to season. The density of some of the relatively unmodified West Coast forests has prompted comparisons with the tropical jungles, a very apt analogy as all who venture far into them will testify.

The vast tussock lands, some extensively modified by the agricultural demands of man, have a charm and rawness which is often equally appealing. The eastern still waters encourage a feeling of freedom and of space to spread, in direct comparison to the intimacy of the forest-shrouded streams further west.

Observers of the natural scene will find plenty to interest them, and to complement the normally superb angling. Back country fishing is a 'total' experience much, much more than just catching fish.

The only way to really appreciate back country angling is to live on location for a time. To really gain a feel for a place it is not sufficient to be whisked in and out of the mountains on a day trip – by helicopter, fixed-wing aircraft, off-road vehicle or jet-boat. The real rewards come to those prepared to steep themselves totally in the environment, preferably by back-packing into a remote location. Accommodation may take the form of simple hut or tent, but nothing can quite compare with the joys of long evenings around a camp fire and the tang of wood smoke in the coffee.

Truly memorable trips are those which combine the elements of good company, top fishing and a smile from the weather gods. Some individual days stand out from the rest. One such occurred for Howard Hill, my brother Terry and myself on a river in North Westland in the summer of 1988/89. After a couple of days of blue skies and moderately successful angling, we elected to back-pack further into the wilderness to a tributary of the main river in an attempt to push further than we had been before. Laden down with tent, utensils and food for a couple of days, we headed out from the hut which had been our base. Determined not to fish until we had reached the stream of our choice we carried our rods in their protective cloth bags and packed the reels away in our packs so as to resist temptations en route.

For the first hour or so that resolve was not broken, but only because our route took us across a broad bush terrace of beech and matai. Before long though we were forced to follow the marked trail out onto the riverbed for a short distance, alongside a deep backwater. Taking a breather, we rested on a large, flat rock and savoured the vista unfolding in front of us. Across the river uniform beech terraces gave way to steeper slopes and a long scree and tussock valley above the tree line. One miniscule patch of old snow clung tenaciously to a south-facing bluff.

All attention though was soon focused on the blue-green backwater. Almost immediately Howard spotted a fish nymphing 60cm or so beneath the surface, right on the transition zone between the still water and the main river current. Within minutes we had seen four – some on station, nymphing, some cruising the backwater on a fixed beat. All resolve not to fish evaporated. Gear was suddenly strewn all over the rocks as rods were hastily assembled.

Howard decided to have a go at a cruiser. Crouching behind a granite boulder, he waited until a portly brown had cruised sedately past and, with the aid of the gentle northerly breeze, wafted a red-tipped governor up in front of the fish. It barely paused to suck in the waiting dry and took without ceremony, arcing the rod in a flurry of spray. After a series of heart-stopping leaps, the trout decided on other tactics and bored down to the very depths of the pool in an attempt to find sanctuary amongst the pale, sharp-edged rocks. Pressure finally took its toll and, undeterred by a possible break-off, Howard soon worked the fish to the surface and into the waiting net. The barbless hook was easily extricated with forceps and the fish, a brown jack of close to 3kg, wobbled off into the depths of the pool.

Terry had his eye on another, and thoughtfully waited until the first fish had been landed before going into action. His fish was lying in the fast water at the top of the run, obviously nymphing. Almost unbelievably it too took on the first drift past, taking a well-weighted stonefly nymph with an unmistakable roll and lift in the water, exposing a broad silver flank. This fish was not content to slug it out in the backwater and made a brave run across the fast water towards the far bank with a burst of speed which took all the floating line and a fair

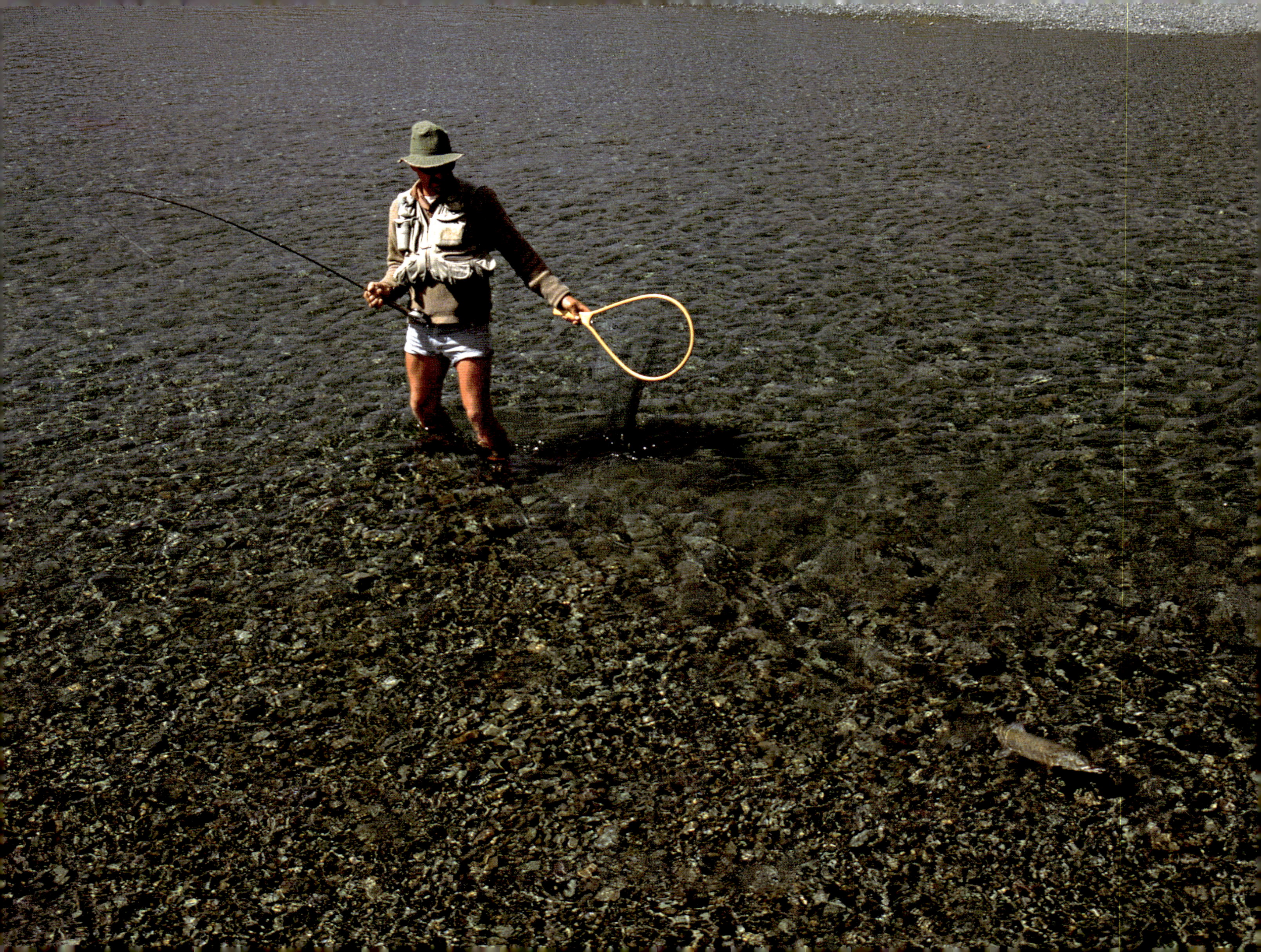

Left:
Success on the Upper Mataura – brown trout water. Clear, gentle, productive.

A brown regaining freedom. The southern rivers draining the high western mountains possess a fragile stock of trout. Releasing fish can only help maintain better numbers and fishing quality.

Wading deep. Larger rivers like the Mokihinui demand an adventurous approach to be fished thoroughly.

proportion of backing within seconds. For some time it sulked behind a large boulder against the far bank, line singing in the current, stretched bow-string tight. For some minutes an impasse prevailed before a broad tail cleaved the surface, preceding a strong dash downstream and back across the current to our side of the river. The sting was certainly out of the fish by this time, and while it fought gamely all the way to the net it was not long before a fish similar to Howard's, resplendent in hundreds of unusually small spots, was on its way back to fight another day.

Then it was my turn. The fish were now decidedly spooked but I was intrigued by a short section of joggly water above the backwater. Cautiously I edged along a steep, unstable shingle bank, careful not to dislodge stones. No fish were visible but the run looked so inviting that I couldn't resist a few casts with a small royal wulff. I was still startled when a head materialised from the broken water. Instinctively I tightened and found myself attached to a lively fish, quite unamused by the deception. This one was smaller but it displayed rare acrobatic ability with nearly a dozen leaps.

It was ten minutes or so before I could lead it down into the backwater to be netted and released in the same place as the others. Smaller maybe, but what a lovely fish. As it lay gasping in the folds of the net I admired the crème de la crème of back country trout, a hen with a small pointed head and huge crimson and black spots over a flank of purest silver. Treasure indeed.

What a start! Incredibly it got better. We packed the rods away and resisted the temptation to fish again until some hours later when we turned off the track up into the 'promised land'. We didn't expect to see fish in abundance in the lower part of the valley, so it was with feelings of pure delight that we spotted three in the first substantial pool, and all of them rising freely to a hatch of small mayflies. Rods and reels reappeared in seconds, and we were back in action. By the time we reached a suitable camp site at seven that evening 13 fish had been landed and released, including one of 3.5kg, a fish of a remarkable golden colouration right to the bottom of its plump belly. This was one of the most memorable of all the hundreds of days I've spent angling in the back country, one to be treasured and stored up in the memory.

That account, correct in every detail, hints at the amazing quality of this fishery. To assume that such scenarios will continue indefinitely is naive though. Despite the literally hundreds of streams and lakes available to the adventurous angler, the fragility of the resource is nothing short of frightening. As I write, forces are massing which pose serious threats to the continued existence of some of the 'jewels in the crown'. One such is an outrageous proposal to divert the headwaters of some of the finest fisheries in the northern South Island via a series of tunnels to feed a massive hydro-electric power scheme at Ngakawau north of Westport. Ironically the Ngakawau itself is in effect already a dead river. Flowing through a magnificent, densely-forested gorge it should sustain a healthy population of brown trout. None are able to survive the grey, lifeless waters poisoned decades ago by the foul leachates from long-abandoned coal mines. The Ngakawau power scheme, so potentially destructive as to be laughable if the proponents were not so deadly serious in their resolve, would ruin the famous Mokihinui Owen and Wangapeka Rivers in addition to drowning thousands of hectares of virgin forest.

Smaller power schemes are also mooted on a whole range of rivers. An irrigation and power scheme on the Branch River in Marlborough, resisted vociferously by Fish and Game Councils and individuals alike, is now a reality, destroying vital trout and salmon spawning habitat. In its place is relatively soulless Lake Argyle and a series of concrete canals. Other local bodies are eyeing up superb small trout streams with mini-hydro schemes in mind.

Also outrageous to many is the plan of Ngai Tahu to develop a monorail or road through the beautiful Greenstone Valley of Otago. A fine brown and rainbow fishery would inevitably suffer seriously from such gross insensitivity in part of the South Westland World Heritage Park and an unspoilt wilderness popular with anglers and trampers. Such a scheme would sound the death knell of the valley's special character and charm.

Many other countries have found to their great cost the price of 'progress' in the form of power schemes, mining, forest clearance and unwise agricultural practices which inevitably bring about degradation of wild trout fisheries. Enough damage has already been done in both main islands of New Zealand. Slowly but surely the wilderness is shrinking. But there is hope. A general world-wide upsurge in interest in things 'green' is having its positive benefits in this

Fun on the Grey. A big river where edge fishing can be most productive – in among the olive, algal-covered boulders.

Miro – Brown Pine
(*Podocarpus ferrungineus*).

110 Images of Silver

Using the shadows. An angler sneaks among some willow trees in pursuit of a shallow water fish on Lake Heron.

country too. Gone are the days of unfettered exploitation of rivers, forests and wetlands. The Ngakawau power proposal will be fought tooth and nail. Once the full implications of such a destructive scheme are made apparent to the general public I have little doubt that it will be treated with the disdain and disgust it deserves. Such a change in attitudes is heartening.

Some perceive other threats. Increased leisure time, greater financial mobility and an upsurge in interest in sports which involve people more and more with the natural environment are booming. Witness the growth of adventure tourism world-wide. New Zealand is no exception. Skiing, white-water rafting, kayaking and fishing are but some of the pastimes which both Kiwis and foreigners are experiencing in ever-increasing numbers.

Despite the thousands of kilometres of water available in the back country, there are few places holding trout which are not visited on a regular basis. Adventurous back-packing anglers and increasing numbers of guided fishermen, visit even the remotest of headwater streams and tiny upland lakes in search of trout, and to experience the true wilderness.

For better or worse this trend will continue. While some see the helicopter as a curse, most thinking anglers are prepared to take a broader view, for it is the people who have been enriched by their experience in the back country who will do the most to preserve it. While agreeing that some areas should remain totally helicopter-free to retain a completely wilderness atmosphere, in most instances the passage of a helicopter or a fixed-wing aircraft is but a temporary intrusion. Aware that they possess a distinct advantage over back-packing anglers, the majority of helicopter pilots and fishing guides take great pains to ensure that they leave adequate water for any party which may already be on the ground. As a guide who frequently uses a helicopter to transport clients to back country streams, I insist that the pilot check carefully for other anglers, and to pull out if there is any possibility of conflict.

Headwater fisheries are very special, and the Professional Fishing Guides Association has recognised that by ear-marking funds from a proposed guides' licence specifically for research and protection.

Already, the unique nature of some streams has been recognised by the imposition of a 'catch and release' policy. It seems certain that more and more no-kill zones will follow.

A backwater fish returned. The term "throwing them back" does not apply to a trout fisherman. Great care should be taken when handling trout.

Images of Silver 113

Happily, most New Zealand anglers who go to the trouble to explore headwater fisheries are committed to 'catch and release', which is a concept easily accepted by the majority of overseas anglers who fish in this country. Indeed, even the suggestion of killing a fish would be sufficient to alarm many anglers. As I have stated elsewhere though it is important not to become too much 'holier than thou' over this issue, and I would resist strongly any attempt to impose a blanket 'no-kill' rule over the bulk of back country waters. Many larger waterways, lakes in particular, can tolerate a moderate harvest of fish, especially those in the smaller, younger classes.

Understandably, most anglers will choose to release their catch without demur, and in the more fragile, mainly headwater streams this practice should be the norm. This is one conservation measure which can be actively participated in by individual anglers, and one which ultimately affords a much greater sense of satisfaction than the sickening thud of a rock on the head of the creature which has afforded so much excitement.

Regrettably, many anglers do not realise that the successful revival of a trout begins from the moment it is hooked. While supporting the use of lightweight rods and lines in order to more easily deceive the fish into taking the fly, it is inexcusable to torture the fish on impossibly light tippets which preclude rapid landing and release. The thrill of being attached to a large, wild trout is one we will never tire of, but the angler should do all in his or her power to ensure that it is brought to the net with as much haste as possible. An active, aggressive approach, once the strong early runs have eased somewhat, will normally succeed. Wherever possible side strain should be applied, placing the fish off balance and forcing it into the edge water relatively quickly. But this can only be achieved with a strong tippet. For most bouldery back country streams I consider 4x tippets to be the absolute minimum. While well aware that it is possible to subdue even the largest and most aggressive of trout with very light tippets in conjunction with a long rod, one wonders what state this leaves the fish in when the victorious angler has departed. On numerous occasions I have observed large eels 'tracking' a hooked trout, and more than once I have had eels attack released fish. One wonders what the mortality rate of exhausted trout is where eels are common as they are in most South Island streams.

In the main, a large, wide-mouthed landing net is an essential item of equipment except on some still waters where it is often less traumatic for the fish to be beached with a steady pull. Where conditions permit, I recommend this method on rivers too. Many back country streams have a zone of sand or fine shingle near the tail of the pool. By keeping well back from the water it is often possible to land a fish before it really realises what has happened. If using barbless hooks (which should be standard equipment), it is a simple matter to flick out the hook, place the fish in an upright position in the current and, without waving it back and forwards, allow it to regain strength and equilibrium.

From my observation of many hundreds of large trout being released it appears that fish go into some form of 'shock' once the violent initial struggles in the net cease. Some would contend that this is caused by a build-up of lactic acid, inducing a form of cramp, such as that well-known to some sportspeople after a strenuous effort. Others argue that removal from the water creates a loss of equilibrium due to an upsetting of the fish's balance mechanism. I would not be surprised to learn that, in fact, both theories are in part correct. The familiar scene of a once wildly struggling trout suddenly taking on a passive, even rigid, mode when it is placed back in the water is one which many anglers will recall, especially when dealing with large trout.

Landing trout, with or without a net, is an art. Undoubtedly two anglers operating as a team can best effect a successful landing and subsequent release. In general a head first approach is easiest, though fraught with peril in very fast water. Many a fish has been lost at the net through becoming entangled in the netting angler's legs or by panicking and breaking off around a rock or other obstruction. Netting is best achieved if the fish is led steadily but firmly to the net. Blind stabs and the pursuit of the fish around the pool simply serve to raise the anxiety level of the fish, possibly resulting in stress mortality after it has been released. We have advocated the inverting of trout in the net once safely enfolded in the mesh. This definitely serves to lessen the possibility of damage to the fish, and enables the hook to be removed swiftly.

Left:
Coming to the net. The hill country rivers of Otago and Southland contrast markedly with their Fiordland and West Otago neighbours.

Fun in northwest Nelson. A dull and showery day, yet a mid-morning mayfly hatch brought trout to the surface.

An Oreti brown about to be returned. The Oreti is a fine river with easy access and a variety of waters.

A fine Taramakau brown – beached but not beaten.

Commonsense should prevail. Obviously, no fish will benefit from thrashing around on hot, dry rocks, having careless fingers thrust into its gills or being squeezed tightly. While the desire to photograph a notable catch is natural, excessive time out of the water could be disastrous. Be prepared by having the camera close to hand, and ensuring that your photographer understands the workings of your camera before a fish is landed.

Wet hands are mandatory when handling trout in order to avoid excessive scale loss. Some advocate the use of cut-off nylon stockings kept wrapped around the wrist. The fine mesh of the stocking enables a firm, non-slip grip on the fish without excessive squeezing. Time should be spent with each fish to ensure that it has the best possible chance of survival. When the fishing is hot the temptation is to move quickly on to the next fish. Spare a thought for the trout. Being left to its own devices prematurely may mean that it has not recovered sufficiently to take care of itself. On a few rare occasions I have observed a seemingly fully recovered trout turn belly up shortly after release. Being left like that will surely result in death. The fish must be held gently, head upstream in moving water. In still waters if is often necessary to revive the fish by 'walking' it forward for some distance. Again, it is incorrect practice to move the fish vigorously back and forward. This can actually drown the fish.

Released trout do survive – providing the release is effected correctly. Those who visit the same waters frequently often encounter the same fish time after time. Indeed some fishing guides refer to some fish by name, recognising familiar physical characteristics and the very precise location of the fish. Despite being caught and landed perhaps five or six times, they usually show no ill effects or significant loss of condition, countering the sometimes-heard argument that released fish will surely die. In the much-fished waters of many U.S. streams, research has proved that some fish are caught and released perhaps dozens of times in one season.

Anglers are generally courteous, considerate people. As interest in our superb back country fisheries grows so too, inevitably, will the potential for conflict. Overcrowding is something all who fish the Taupo waters in winter know only too well. Despite the excellence of the fishing in the Tongariro when the rainbows are running I personally find the overall scene there stressful and highly competitive. In recent years some South Island gems have suffered from the same malaise, especially on the opening weekend of the season. Regrettably the manners of some on the prime North Island waters have often left a great deal to be desired. I have personally experienced boorish behaviour unbecoming to any outdoor sportsman. Here I make a plea for consideration for the rights of others. Helicopter-borne anglers should consider those who may have walked for days into a prime fishery. Similarly, it is inexcusable to deliberately leapfrog another party without prior consultation. If more than one party is on the same water, it is encumbent upon all to sort out a strategy which allows all concerned a fair and equitable share of the available fishing.

As has been stressed earlier, this book is a plea for the preservation of one of the world's greatest sports fishing locations. Please, please, enjoy, admire and respect so that future generations may do so too.

Bibliography

Trout and Salmon of the World, Silvio Calabi, The Wellfleet Press.

Meadow, Mountain, Forest and Stream, The Provincial History of The Nelson Acclimatisation Society 1863-1968, W.C.R. Sowman, Nelson Acclimatisation Society.

The New Zealand Encyclopaedia of Fly Fishing, Bryn Hammond, The Halcyon Press.

Stalking Trout, Les Hill and Graeme Marshall, The Halcyon Press.

Catching Trout, Les Hill and Graeme Marshall, The Halcyon Press.